To Philip

Enjoy the journey

Best wishes

John

To my wife, Josiane, love of my life.

Thank you for your inspiration

and support for this book.

This is Paradise!

Mount Rainier, Washington State USA with Reflection Lake in foreground

(shutterstock)

Foreword

Colin Speakman, Author and Environmentalist

This is a very different kind of travel book. John Davies is both a career railwayman and man with passions - for railways, for travel, for people, for good food and, as well as his native Wales, for the many countries in mainland Europe and North America he has travelled through over a very active lifetime.

Unlike most of us, John also recorded his trips - 100,000 'surface miles' across mainland Europe and 55,000 in North America - using both an accurate memory and his camera. So what we have, between Hell and Paradise, is a remarkable record of travel experiences recorded within space and time - starting in his teenage years in the late 1950s on a first school trip to France, to serious explorations as a young man journeying independently or with close friends for business and pleasure in the 1970s and 80s, a time when many European rural railways were still scruffy and rundown after the Second World War. But he also records the period of rapid change in the 90s and into the present century, ending - at least for the purpose of the book - in some epic, more recent trips through Northern Europe and North America.

His earlier journeys offer an important historic record, coinciding as they did with the last years of steam in Germany and France, and indeed into the early years of preservation in Europe and North America, with journeys behind some of the last great steam giants but also first- generation diesels and classic electric traction, together with records of journeys on some of the most romantic narrow-gauge lines of Europe.

There is much to delight the transport enthusiast in this book, especially from the pen of someone who as a professional railwayman understands the technical and operational aspects of railways. It also has much to interest the more general reader sharing a love of travel to some of the most fascinating countries and regions in Europe and North America.   There are some sad moments, such as last journeys behind particular locomotives or diesel or electric units soon to be withdrawn or on lines soon to be closed. But there is also a great deal of fun and humour, as our sharp-eyed author-guide takes a wry and sometimes even slightly cynical look at the rapidly changing world of railways, urban transport and tourist travel. When it is sensible to do so, John abandons the train for the plane and if necessary, the hire car to get to those special places - but he is never far from an interesting main line or branch railway.

Overall John captures much of the joy of travel and discovery of the countries he especially loves - France, the home of his beloved and constant travelling companion Josiane - Italy, 'Spectacular' Spain, Germany, Scandinavia up to the Arctic circle, and a glorious celebration of some of the epic trans-continental journeys they made together across the USA and Canada. But there are also chapters offering the reader time to enjoy the essence some of the great cities of Europe and North America from stations and railway lines.

Because the book is structured around specific countries and places, not dates of visits, in a single chapter you may move from the elderly semi-streamlined diesel express locomotive traction of the 1980s to the latest sleek Spanish AVE high speed sensation. That is one of its delights and makes it a book to constantly dip into, a perfect bedside companion.

The splendid photographs, some taken from a railway carriage window or veranda, not only reflect half a century of European and American rail traveL but offer stunning images of some of the great landscape of the world only accessible by train, surely the most romantic and satisfying form of travel on earth.

And where was Hell (where John jokingly confesses he was only offered a single ticket to) and where was Paradise? You will have to read this book to find out.

Colin Speakman

We've all probably been on the train from hell at some time, but what about going *to* Hell on a one-way ticket! Or arriving at Paradise twenty years on and finding it's not much different... That is probably why I felt I should do penance in Purgatory yet another twenty-two years later! How about a lightning 20-minute visit to Las Vegas at 8 in the morning; staying in Chattanooga and Kalamazoo, both featuring in Glenn Miller's Big Band repertoire; and following in the footsteps of fictional Monsignor Quixote in Spain or Inspector Montalbano in Sicily? And the really scary one; Josiane and I outside the twin towers in New York one year to the day before 9/11! None of this would have been in my mind on my school trip to France in 1958 which was to start a lifelong love of travel that would take me through Europe and North America.

Some are born to travel - others have travel thrust upon them - and there are those who fall into travel as a way of life; it is the latter into which I fit. Important influences in my early years and schooldays were to guide me. My father was a prolific traveller though only in mainland Britain during my early days. I took to Geography in school and was lucky to have an interested and supportive teacher, gaining a distinction in the subject at 'A Level'. I learned about interesting places throughout the World and wanted to see for myself.

My story takes the reader on what I like to term 'travel adventures' (every journey is an adventure) and I relate high and low points, people, places and humorous interludes. It starts in 1958 when I join a group of 5th and 6th formers from Neath Grammar School on a trip to Menton on the French Riviera. My motivation is to see what this foreign country is like, enjoy new experiences - particularly travel - with a bonus of sunshine, sand and sea. The long journey over two days and nights is a thrill, and I savour the difference as I step onto French soil at Calais and at our destination, an exotic Italianate town on the French Riviera. I follow this with another school trip to Paris a year later.

My narrative is written mostly in the present tense to convey a sense of being there and I adopt the maxim 'the tourist sees what he has come to see; the traveller sees what he sees' *(G.K. Chesterton)*.

Top: Josiane and John outside the French Senate

The next sixty years will see me at the Russian frontier in the north of Norway and the ancient ruins of Olympia at the other end of Europe; visiting the romantic cities of Santa Fe and Charleston in the USA, and the World Heritage towns of Ragusa and Quedlinburg in Europe. I even outdo Chris Tarrant on my extreme railway journey in Alaska (and tell him face to face)*. And the train journeys to die for through France's Massif central or up the Pacific coast of the USA on the *Coast Starlight*; unknowingly sharing a sleeper cabin with a criminal on the *Night Ferry*; and listening to a researchers' tales of the great Wild West pioneer trails whilst travelling through the night on the *Southwest Chief*.

*at his book signing 'Extreme Railway Journeys' in the Hay Literary Festival 2017

It is to be twelve years before my European horizons expand beyond France and a further twenty years before discovering North America - my visit there results from a happy accident - given a previous antipathy to the USA. In 1977, I was shortlisted for a Rotary-sponsored twinning visit to South Dakota and failed to secure a place which got me thinking that maybe I should go anyway. Close friend, Paul - with whom I had travelled adventurously in southern Europe and return through two Communist countries - agreed to join me on my first trip across the Atlantic in 1978. The rest is history as we become instant converts to the new continent and I for one make a further eight visits, covering 47 States, though South Dakota is not among them!

And the significance of the title? I go to Hell before Paradise and that it's that way round may speak volumes. Did I redeem myself? Strangely, as recently as 2015, I am to find myself in Purgatory (the *Church of Anime Sante del Purgatorio* in Ragusa, Sicily - chap. 8) so perhaps I needed a refresh!

Hell is on the Norwegian coast and as near to a paradise as one could imagine. Paradise is in Mount Rainier National Park in Washington State, USA and, had events taken a different turn in 1980, could have become Hell (nearby Mount St Helen's blew its top in spring of that year).

As with my feelings of elation on reaching the summit of a great mountain, I experience similar on arrival at Calais in 1958; travelling unscathed through communist countries in 1977; arriving in New York in 1978; and in reaching Anchorage, Alaska after 48 hours semi-continuous travel in 1988.

If you like statistics, mine are amazing: 100,000 surface miles travelled in mainland Europe and 55,000 in North America (with international flights accounting for a lot more miles)

These experiences form the basis of this book and my objective is to share them with my readers. Most of my travels are accompanied, over the past 25 years by my wife, Josiane and previously, by various friends, who I refer to by their first names.

Shiprock, New Mexico (author)

EUROPE

My first impressions of Europe are formed in France at the tender age of fifteen and I soon find out how little I know about that country, let alone about the rest of the continent. However, I revel in the differences to my own country rather than try to understand them.

France suffered more from the Second World War than the UK and it shows in most places though I don't notice it so much on the Côte d'Azur because I'm mesmerised by the sun-soaked atmosphere and food I can only dream of back home. Paris surprisingly is rather ordinary outside the city centre and many of the buildings have peeling plaster and dull grey slatted window shutters (something completely new to me). Peoples' dress sense, though, is superior to ours and it's something I continue to notice about France in particular.

As to other European countries, each one I visit prompts a reappraisal of my impressions as all are different, some in more subtle ways than others. Germany, Switzerland and the Netherlands exude prosperity; Italy and Spain strike me as fun-loving countries with a casual attitude to work and life; and I perceive the Nordic countries as taking life more seriously.

There are no European countries where I do not feel welcome and I speak here of the ordinary people I come into contact with, or who serve me at hotels, shops, and travelling. The exception is with officialdom, particularly in Greece, Spain and Communist countries of Yugoslavia and Hungary. It is often unpleasant at border crossings and police can be a major irritant. Things get better with the Schengen 'no borders' Europe (except the UK of course!) and the fall of the 'iron curtain', though old habits die hard in former East Germany. In general, people all over are basically decent though every nation has its bad eggs.

I warm to nearly all of the capital and major cities in European countries which universally exude growing confidence as they shake off the relics of wartime and most pay a lot of attention to their heritage. There are big differences between Spain and Italy, Spain giving more care and attention to honouring their history whereas Italy displays its heritage with neglect. That is to change in the 25 years separating my visits to Florence which cleans up dramatically though Venice has always looked good. German cities are largely re-built from their wartime ruins where a sense of order dominates aesthetics.

One thing that surprises me is differences in the rural landscape, towns and villages, Germany most of all, where much seems untouched by war and many towns and villages are half-timbered and rustic. Spain is at the opposite end appearing to be largely devoid of rural settlements seen in most other countries. France and Italy both have lots of small towns and villages, many hugging mountainsides (a relic of when they served as defences). In the Nordic countries, I notice places are more colourful than elsewhere particularly the walls and roofs of buildings. In Belgium and the Netherlands, settlements are closer to what I am used.

A big difference is with travel, most of which I do by train. European rail systems vary greatly in quality of service. German, Swiss and Austrian trains are good and customer service satisfactory if rather impersonal. Spain and Italy are rather chaotic and improvements come slowly; Spanish trains are hideously difficult to use which is why coach travel is so prevalent in that country. In France, trains live up to only one of the SNCF strapline slogans: *Exactitude*; with *Confort*, well, they just don't get it; and *Vitesse* mainly available to those that can afford it! Over time, things get better though the biggest improvements come with the new high speed lines and services whilst other routes languish. Urban transit is everywhere publicly owned, highly regulated and, with notable exceptions, fails to move fast enough with the times. Rural public transport is poor in France, Italy and Spain. Trams are prevalent in the main towns and cities, particularly in north central Europe and later in France and Spain. Coaches outside the Iberian Peninsula are few and far between, highly regulated to protect railways from competition.

The south coast of Brittany has some superb resorts: Benodet in Finistére

NORTH AMERICA

Visiting America twenty years later, at the age of thirty five, I might have been expected to know at least a bit more. I did, but that didn't stop me getting a massive culture shock particularly as most of my previously held thoughts (let's call them this rather than prejudices) are in tatters within days of my arrival.

From being one of America's greatest sceptics, I become an ardent enthusiast (forget politics; I refer to the country and its people). I find big differences between Canada and the USA and initially veer to the former as it feels more akin to what I am used. That is to change even before the end of my first visit as the USA attracts more. Why? Because it is so different - its biggest plus is a 'can do' attitude - so refreshing when I've been used to years of the opposite back home, where there is often resistance to new ideas and an inability to pick up quickly when things go wrong. The differences diminish as the years roll on, quite possibly due to people seeing how the USA's less regulated environment could work here. However, the USA does appear backward in technical development, for example, in design of cars and televisions, it seems to lag well behind even British practice.

In Canada and USA alike, the welcome is good and most people are very open. I find that extraordinary service doesn't usually have to be requested, it's a given. However, I have to be on my guard as there are quite a lot of people who will look you in the eye and rip you off; *caveat emptor*.

My preconceptions about the cities are substantially correct in 1978; with a few exceptions I wouldn't write home about them and the deference to the motor car is complete in many to the detriment of their ambience. That changes radically over the 22 years between my first and last visit.

The countryside, particularly New England, the Rocky Mountain states and the west coast has some stunning land and seascapes, equal to any I have seen in Europe. The wide-open spaces - 'big sky country' - I find particularly attractive.

Travel is different to anywhere else that I've experienced and it takes time to adapt to this completely new scenario. What appears on a map to be a reasonable distance usually turns out to be much greater. Having opted to do most travel by train, the first obstacle seems to be that many places are no longer served this way. The good news is that in both countries there is a semblance of a national network, together with good value period 'anywhere' tickets. One adapts, filling in network gaps by renting a car or using the *Greyhound* bus. Car rental is less bureaucratic and more competitive than in Europe; one is able to haggle on price or threaten to shop around. It usually works though in Tampa, Florida, I'm sold a low base price plus a low rate per mile and end up with a huge bill due to the mileage travelled; *caveat emptor* again!

Roads are generally good though it takes some getting used to the general 55 mph maximum speed on open highways; even the police are often polite (none of this *'shift your ass'*) when I have roadside checks though I do get a warning ticket from Florida Highway Patrol for running a flashing red light; the female officer looks like film star Shirley MacLaine and she may have been lenient when she finds I am Welsh as she's been to my country and likes it.

So I give America an 'A star'!

The police aren't the only hazard awaiting us on the roads of Florida!

Travel

There has always been something special to me about a journey and particularly on a train. I have been fortunate over my adult lifetime to enjoy travelling to the ends of the European continent either free or relatively cheaply and this has broadened my horizons.

So it is interesting to look at the situation of travel in Europe over the years. Outside the UK, all railway companies are publicly owned with private enterprise at the margins in some countries. Most other public transport is also publicly owned except airlines and coaches. Transport is largely integrated in most countries though often there is little co-ordination between modes other than lip service being paid.

I travel to and through nineteen European countries, effectively the whole of former Western Europe and including four former communist states.

The State of Public Transport

My first impressions formed in 1958/59 as a schoolboy in France for the first time are of a system picking

Left: Köln Hauptbahnhof (Cologne Central Station) is one of the major railway hubs of Europe. I am impressed by the German intercity network which generally runs at hourly frequency with cross-platform interchange at hubs like this. The intercity locomotives and livery are very iconic (author)

itself up from the ravages of war. This applies across the spectrum of trains and buses and exemplified by the amount of rolling stock that is outdated. There is a lot of investment into the railways in particular (electrification and infrastructure) though buses seem to be largely left out of these plans. That is to change but the impression I form, first in France, is that modernisation of assets proceeds apace without a corresponding change of attitude to service provision.

It is another eleven years before I can start assessing my thoughts about other railway systems. My travel horizons broaden, first to the Netherlands, Germany and Switzerland followed by Austria and the Nordic countries then Spain and finally, Italy and Greece.

Early on, there is a noticeable north-south divide, with transport better organised and customer friendly in central and northern Europe. Recent times have seen a levelling up as Spain and Italy improve a great deal with their high-speed networks. I have no recent experience of Greece though hear things are not good. The pervading feeling over the years is that public transport is considered more of a commodity than a commercial undertaking and this influences thinking. The speed and quality of trains, design and organisation of bus networks has improved greatly but while specification largely remains in government hands, innovation will be patchy. This is a reason why train travel grows faster in the UK than the rest of Europe.

Left: Germany is probably the European country where tram systems are most prolific, with every city and large town of note having networks. Whilst those in West Germany have seen extensive modernisation, little has changed in East Germany under communism. *Tatra*-built trams operate in towns and cities all over ex-Soviet countries including in the beautiful city of Dresden (author)

I am an enthusiastic supporter of trams, more often referred to as light rapid transit. In many European countries, they form the backbone of urban transit systems and in others, notably France and Spain, there is a renaissance with even relatively small cities having networks; a lot of this has been politically driven.

Only once do I use a long-distance coach on the continent - in 1971 between Landeck, Austria and Scuols, Switzerland - a means of getting over the Alps where no railway exists. Operated by *Europabus*, a company running across borders between railways - and funded by participating countries - is a publicly regulated service and very useful though long since confined to history. As for long distance coaches in general, they are for years non-existent as most countries protect their rail services from competition. Only in Spain, Portugal and some former Communist countries are coaches significant transport providers. The same policy applies to internal air services, again limited in scope for the same reasons as coaches. This changes in many European countries as EU regulations force competition, bringing multi-country coach operator *Flixbus* and airline *EasyJet* operating internal European routes.

Passenger comfort is important in generating travel and initial impressions in France are unfavourable, most carriages having hard green leather seats; this changes for the better in the 1970's with introduction of the *Corail* (*confort-rail*), which extends over France and still extant though now cascaded to regional service. In Germany of the 1970's the standard intercity carriage rides beautifully though seating is a bit spartan. They seem to be the norm in other central European railways and its design reigns supreme for years.

The introduction of high-speed trains brings a complete revamp of carriage interiors, which generally retain high standards of comfort. The same cannot always be said about new multiple-unit rolling stock for regional services where comfort is often compromised for capacity reasons.

Incidents

Not surprisingly, my two school trips in the late 1950's have their share of incidents. At Paris Gare de Lyon on our journey to the south of France, some boys bait ticket collectors (looking very Gallic in their tams) freely using four letter words until one retorts: *'please speak more slowly, I don't understand English!'* Next day at Marseille station, I experience being 'done' by a mobile refreshment vendor selling ice creams, great on a stifling hot day. He speaks little English; I lean out of the window, hand over precious francs, and he walks away without giving change!

In 1971 I am at Milan Central station on a family holiday and we split up to do the return journey by alternative routes. My father agrees to get tickets for mother and sister to travel direct to Brussels. A long queue is slow moving and an American is getting agitated; an Italian 'heavy' promises to break into the queue for which he is handed a wad of dollars. The Italian barges in, a fight ensues and the American loses his money!

On 6 December 1996, accompanied by Josiane and daughter Nathalie, I travel to Paris on *Eurostar*. Nothing special in that except it is two days after reopening of service following the Channel Tunnel fire in October.

Left: Gare du Nord in Paris is terminus for *Eurostar* trains from London Waterloo. In the late '90's it is still a rather cramped facility; the welcome is often muted and can actually get quite unfriendly as noted below. French officialdom doesn't take kindly being proved wrong! (*shutterstock*)

Eurostar runs a restricted schedule, passenger use is light and we get exceptional service, including automatic upgrade to first class from staff *so* pleased to see us again. On our return two days later, there are two departures thirty minutes apart, Josiane and I booked on the first, and Nathalie the second. We ask a stewardess at Gare du Nord if we can travel together as we believe there to be plenty of seats; the answer, an emphatic NON; we must travel as booked as there are no spare seats! My brother-in-law remonstrates in colourful French and, overhearing the exchange, a supervisor calls us over and quietly makes the change!

People

There are few problems in dealing with ordinary people in host countries though it can be different with officials, mainly in Communist and Fascist countries. My impressions are mainly favourable and language difficulties are solved with smiles and apologies … attempting some of the native language usually works.

In 1994, Josiane and I stay in Tours and book a coach tour of the Loire Chateaux. It's about one-third full and we have a relaxing journey with a pleasant, well-informed driver. We start at Chinon, furthest from Tours and work back; Chinon is the largest chateau and I find it less interesting than the others. Here, I recall learning a new French phrase in the coach park, when our driver is cut up by a young lady in a 2CV and he is angered by this and shouts *'merde alors'*, which Josiane tells me is very rude!

Interesting travel companions

Conversation between strangers doesn't come naturally to many Europeans as I find it does in the USA; the language barrier is sometimes to blame; however, I get some interesting experiences in my travels. Lots of conversations over the years are with young people on grand tour of Europe using an *InterRail* Pass. This facility appeals to people from all over the world and is wonderful for promoting contact between people.

On my first visit to Norway with Chris, on the ferry, we get into conversation over dinner with a young lady travelling to meet her fiancée who she expects to marry soon, and is very excited. A year later as I queue in London Liverpool Street for the boat train to Harwich, by amazing coincidence, there in front of me is the very same young lady. She is as surprised as I and confirms she did marry, introduces her husband, and they are off to Holland where they now live!

In 1972, I'm on a cross-country train between Hagen and Kassel in Germany; in my compartment, I get into conversation with a professor from Switzerland. Recognising my Welsh accent, he tells me he goes to Wales often and is friendly with a reverend in Neath who just happens to be my local parish priest and it seems his reputation for rudeness, which I have experienced, is widely known in Europe!

I travel on the *Night Ferry* through sleeper between London and Paris several times. On one such journey, accompanied by my father, a mistake in berth allocation finds us booked in different coaches and I share my cabin with a stranger. He boards with a large, long cardboard carton which only just fits on to the rack above the upper berth. I think little more about it until Dunkerque where we are woken for a customs inspection. An officer shouts *agent commercial* and as a sales representative, assume it's me but it is the

other man they are after; they check papers and passport, insist the carton comes down, take it in the corridor and rip it open. Police arrive and escort him at gunpoint; at the start of my holiday I witness a criminal arrest!

Left: Wagons-Lits sleepers look out of place in London Victoria; a smart exterior livery and appearance belies spartan interior décor and comfort below expectations (*Eastbank mrc*)

On one of our *Eurostar* journeys between London and Paris, Josiane and I find ourselves sitting across the aisle from former MP Neil Kinnock, at that time, European Commissioner for Transport. I can't resist speaking to him and find him amiable. An opinion from him (to Josiane's dismay) is that the problem with attracting cross-channel freight to rail is France and SNCF's lack of interest; and with tongue in cheek, he says it would have been better if the tunnel exit was in Spain!

Off-beat Europe

On my first visit to Brittany in 1964, I am on a train from Quimper for the 6½ hour journey to Le Mans, steam-hauled by a mighty *Mountain class* locomotive with 19 coaches. On board is a woman whose sole task is cleaning handrails contaminated with fine dust from burning low-quality coal in the locomotive; by the time she reaches the final coach she is back to square one and has to start all over again.

On my 1972 Scandinavia holiday with Chris, we are on a local train from Boden in Sweden to Tornio in Finland to connect to Oulu, a two hour wait. At a buffet on the station we get refreshment and ask the young lady server what there is to do in the time. *'You can play the Yuke (sic) Box'*; so we do, and top of the charts in Finland 1972? *Those were the days my friends* from one-hit star Mary Hopkin from South Wales!

I'm in Greece with Paul in 1977 and take a train to Olympia to see the ancient ruins of the original Olympic Stadium, a short walk from the station. We are surprised to find this internationally famous site in a run-down condition. The intense heat of early afternoon makes it difficult to explore but we persevere and are pleased to do so as it is one of the most important historical places in the World. We expect it to be crowded, but there are only modest numbers of visitors; maybe it is the wrong time of day (*mad dogs and Englishmen go out in the midday sun*: Noel Coward).

Above: remains of the original Olympic stadium (author)

I am with Josiane on a trip to Normandy in 1997, *Eurostar* to Lille then by car. The journey to Rouen is a drag through the industrial Nord region and as we come upon the town of St-Pol-sur-Ternoise, Josiane gasps. She is teaching French at Swansea Institute and one of her textbooks has a chapter on a 'typical' medium-sized French town based on St-Pol, whereupon her previous rose tinted view turns to horror!

Work-related Europe

In the 1970's as a rail freight sales and marketing executive I have interesting anecdotes of Europe. In 1972 with colleague Stan, we visit the Harwich-Zeebrugge train ferry operation. After being hosted to lunch by the Port Manager for Ostend where I drink rather well, he drops us at Zeebrugge in early evening and we meet the crew of the *Cambridge Ferry* for the return trip; dine with the captain and crew followed by whiskies, then taken to the bridge for departure. The captain invites me to steer the ship out of port, wisely standing behind me, and I achieve it successfully. Months later, a RO/RO ferry, *Herald of Free Enterprise* rolls right over on departure from Ostend with tragic consequences and a chill goes through me!

Sometimes, events in my work are quite baffling; you couldn't make them up! Such a time relates to the time when, having struck up a relationship with Spanish wagon company *Transfesa*, whose vans I contract to carry tinplate from west Wales to Spanish canning factories. Their inwards traffic of fruit and vegetables is highly seasonal and there are lean times when they have numerous surplus vans.

When I negotiate a very large contract to convey cans and can ends from *Metal Box* factories in Worcester and Neath to a canner in Poland for *'erbsen grunen'* (green peas), I turn to *Transfesa* to supply vans and they're happy to oblige. The first consignment is stopped at the Polish border which I think may be due to wrong paperwork. The reason, however, is blatantly political; apparently, the Polish government are furious that vans from a fascist country are being used to convey traffic to their communist country, so the cargo is transhipped at the border and the remainder takes several months due to the shortage of normal vans.

In 1979, on a rail tour of the Netherlands including a visit to the Ijmuiden steelworks, I travel in a vintage train hauled by a steam locomotive; a p.a. system on the train explains what is being seen. I know a lot about integrated strip rolling mills having recently finished a spell as a freight marketing executive based at Port Talbot works; it is smaller than Ijmuiden and 'straight' whereas this is 'circular' though with identical processes and activities. All enjoy a great trip but don't understand what is being said so those around me are impressed by my explanation of activities and processes which mirror those at Port Talbot. I don't let on about my 'insider' knowledge and let them think I'm translating!

Right: the vintage *Stoomtren* (steam train) owned by Hoogovens is used to transport visitors around their steelworks at Ijmuiden. Here it is approaching the coke ovens, a fact I know from my own experience. The public address is a novelty though the narrative is in Dutch (author)

In late 1982, as sales and marketing manager for East Anglia I am invited on a travel agents facility visit to sample the new TGV in France. After a reception in Paris hosted by TV personality David Jacobs, we travel down the main line to Moret where the inaugural *Ligne a Grand Vitesse* starts and runs to a point near Lyon. As we join the new line our conductor announces in halting English: *'ladies and gentlemen, fasten your seat belts, we are about to take off and travelling at 300 kph'*. The train surges forward quickly reaching maximum speed on an amazing gradient profile with very sharp ascents and descents.

Hotels, food and drink

Left: The attractive Normandy seaside town of Le Treport is the first place I stay as an independent traveller in France. The one-star hotel there and years later the small hotel on Veynes station in the French Alps (where I am forced to stay due to strike action) have four-star style restaurants. In both cases the accommodation is very basic and I am fazed at Le Treport by the lack of even a wash basin in the room. How come the restaurants are so much better than the rooms? The explanation lies in the tax breaks for restaurants if they supply accommodation so why spend money on that! (author)

In spring 1971 I am with my parents arriving in Vienna and our train is running late. There is a hotel booking bureau in the station, just as well as the city is full, and we accept whatever we can get. The hotel is a large gaunt building with heavy oak door and iron bell-pull. We ring, an old lady appears in the dim light and shows us to our room, via another room occupied by a young American couple; we assure them we will knock before entering their room in the morning! We have booked two nights and encounter no problems!

Eating out in style is part of a good holiday and I have my share of anecdotes of experiences, good and bad.

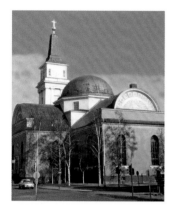

My first experience of being unable to read a menu written only in the native language is at Oulu in Finland in 1972 on my visit with Chris. The menu is written entirely in Finnish, though the server is able to help us a little even though he has little English. It's *Borscht* (beetroot soup) for starter and Reindeer Steak and Chips for the main course, both of which we enjoy. Oulu is a Russian style city that Chris opines looks as if it's from the set of *Doctor Zhivago*!

Above: the Russian Orthodox cathedral at Oulu is built in a *heavy* style typical of this city (author)

Right: eating a great train meal with an outside view like this is magic! The *Iberia Express* south of Bilbao (author)

I enjoy a meal on the train and my first in Spain more than compensates for our lousy initial experiences of Spanish Railways in 1975. My father and I are on the *Iberia Express* from Bilbao to Burgos and the train conveys a restaurant car where meals are cooked on a coke-fired range. Despite this uniquely difficult method of cooking in a confined kitchen, the meal is delicious and the price reasonable, an excellent start to our appreciating Spanish cuisine at its best.

Later that week, we are in the *Ramblas*, Barcelona's principal tourist area and on the menu at dinner in the restaurant is *Paella de Valencia*, which we've not heard of let alone seen before. Cooked in front of us on a central range, chicken and seafood is added to a mountain of saffron rice with squid and octopus legs a final embellishment. Eaten with some trepidation, we are amazed at how delicious it is. I haven't had *Paella* as good as this since.

In 1979, Peter and I are ending a grand tour of Europe at Calais where we arrive too late for a decent ferry link so check in at a new style of budget hotel *Formule 1*; this is by credit card which gets us a key card for a small bedroom that resembles a prison cell. It doesn't take long to decide this ought to be renamed *Formule 0*, so we forgo the low rate levied on our card and seek a proper hotel; a nice B&B on the seafront.

In 1971, my father and I are in Albi in south-west France. Before visiting its massive cathedral, we lunch in a café run by an old lady who is very welcoming and suggests her *terrine maison* as a speciality; it comes in a large bowl, we are told to help ourselves which we do, polishing off most of it. But this is just a starter and we're full so have no main course. We are profusely apologetic but she will have none of it.

Left: Albi is an amazing city, near Toulouse in south-west France. Well before one arrives, its red sandstone cathedral looms large. It is not only tall but its walls are the thickest of any cathedral, the reason being that it had a dual purpose of worship and defence. It was built in the 13th century as defence against the *Cathars* (author)

In the blazing summer of 2003, Josiane and I are driving from Provence to Toulouse and stop in Narbonne. It is impossible to get a room and we eventually stay at a roadside *auberge* west of the city run by two gentlemen who serve the most fantastic meals. The reason the city is full becomes clear next day when the *Tour de France* comes to town. It's a great spectacle though heavily commercialised; in the morning is a parade of sponsors; and the cyclists set off after lunch when it is 40 degrees! *Right*: Tour de France riders contend with the heat! *(shutterstock)*

Bureaucracy

As noted above, there are few problems in dealing with ordinary people in host countries though the situation can be very different dealing with officialdom, particularly in Communist and Fascist countries. My impressions of people are otherwise overwhelmingly favourable and language difficulties are often sorted with smiles and apologies.

Above: TER arrives at Miranda de Ebro (author)

On my first visit to Spain with my father, alighting at Irun, the choice is not only four onward trains but four classes of service and four ticket office queues (a different price for each train)! A sign of those times is that most things public in Spain are very bureaucratic and make little sense to the traveller. Multiple ticket offices are a feature of most large stations; forewarned is forearmed and we don't make the same mistake again! We are not going far so opt for the lowest price which we assume is for the smart diesel railcar we see waiting; it isn't; our train is a TER (*Tren Espreso Regional*) through to Vigo in Galicia and we pay a supplement for the 180 km journey to Miranda de Ebro.

Instances of open hostility are experienced in 1977 when Paul and I travel independently through Yugoslavia and Hungary. Border controls are tedious, armed police patrol the trains and there is a close call just inside Hungary when I see a steam locomotive with a red star on its boiler door. As I get my camera out, an armed policeman enters the corridor and Paul goes ballistic. I wisely return the camera to my bag and no more is said. The previous day our train from Greece arrives late at Belgrade and the Budapest connection has gone so we need to find accommodation. First stop is the station buffet where we order coffee which comes in what resembles an oilcan with liquid the consistency of crude oil and tasting of very strong coffee; it clears our heads! On enquiry, we are told of a state travel agency outside the station named *Putnik*. Sub-consciously, I look upwards outside expecting to see a hovering satellite but no, there is a *Putnik* across the road. It is a café and the server there has a problem of communication due to language, so I resort to sign language with a slumber symbol and she 'twigs' and points me next door to a travel shop of the same name!

Super Service

On occasions I experience service out of the ordinary and as so often it is small things that impress; as when I take a number 20 bus from St Lazare to the Marais in Paris. It travels narrow streets with a local clientele and the driver, knowing his customers, greets us with a gushing *Messieurs Dames, Bonjour!!*

It is summer 1970 and one of those long weary travel days where nothing goes to plan. My father and I arrive at the town of Rodez in late evening by rail-link bus. The station is a bit out of town and our driver kindly stops by the *Hotel de la Poste* in the centre, a hotel I will remember for ever. We are checked in personally by the manager who asks if we wish to have dinner. It is an excellent meal, and we realise on leaving the restaurant that all the kitchen and serving staff have been kept on just for us!

In the first few years of my marriage to Josiane, we fly regularly from Cardiff to Paris CDG in 29-seater *Jetstream 41* planes operated by Manx Air. On my first journey, I need the toilet and the stewardess has to get her bags out before I go into a tiny cabin which appears to be sticking out from the fuselage (imagine the advert: *hot and cold running water and outside toilet!)* it's amazing how they fit it all in.

Above: a *Jetstream 41* at Cardiff Airport in 1995   *Above right*: Rodez Cathedral opposite Hotel de La Poste (author)

Two years later it's still a *Jetstream* and I ask the steward if I might be permitted a few minutes with the pilots; this is agreed. I enter as the plane is flying over northern France; the pilots are friendly and explain the controls. We are close to Paris CDG and they allow me to stay as long as I keep quiet. Over Pontoise, west of CDG we turn and come in from the east to land. Always apprehensive about landing, after seeing it done, it looks a piece of cake and my fears subside.

I suppose it had to happen and in 2011 in Paris it does; on a routine weekend visit a public services strike is announced and we have challenges in getting to CDG on Monday morning. The *Air France* coach is running from Montparnasse and we get a taxi to the air terminal there. On arrival at CDG we find to our horror that air traffic control is also on strike and the Cardiff flight is cancelled. Our only option is to get to Gare du Nord and take our chances on *Eurostar* but no coaches operate anywhere near there. The RATP *Roissybus* goes through La Chapelle, a kilometre from Gare du Nord and the driver kindly agrees to detour though is anxious his management doesn't find out. After this good turn, the next problem is to find seats on *Eurostar*. To our surprise we are offered two first-class tickets on the next departure and there is a discount promotion that day; just 15 Euros each including meals. On boarding, our hostess says we can't expect to be served meals with a discount ticket, but I point out that *all* first-class tickets entitle one to a meal. That's not good enough for her and she cites two men sitting opposite who have paid over 100 Euros for their tickets. Sides are taken, one agrees with the steward, the other with me and Josiane intervenes speaking in French to get common sense. Our host wrongly agrees 'as a special case' and we get our meals.

On an Auvergne holiday with Josiane, we travel through the volcanic mountain region and detour to the village of St Nectaire. This delightful place gives its name to a famous brand of French cheese and we visit the farm where it's made; a large enterprise, completely rural and they show us the cows, milking shed and the bull whose name is *Asterix*!

Left: the small village of St Nectaire in the Cantal Département is well known for its abbey and its celebrated cheese *(shutterstock)*

Cantal is famed for its agricultural produce of which beef and cheese is prominent. *St Nectaire* is a soft cheese and there is a noted hard cheese simply named *Cantal;* top of the range in this genre is *Salers*, a very tangy cheese produced in a rustic village of the same name; we go there as well.

Where in France is this place?

No matter to which town or city I go in France, there is always a sign to 'Toutes Directions'. The place doesn't appear on any maps yet it must be very important! So, where is it? In summer 2003 I find the answer when I arrive at Auch in the Gers region of southwest France. The little bus takes us from the station to the hilltop town (incidentally, it is the birthplace of the *Three Musketeers*) out by one route and back by another and nowhere do I see a sign to 'Toutes Directions'. Eureka, this must be it!

France is the first European country I visit as far back as 1958 on a school trip to Menton on the Côte d'Azur, followed in 1959 by another school trip to Paris. These are to be pivotal in my great love of France long before I visit any other European countries.

Thirty-seven years later, my attachment to France is further strengthened by marriage to Josiane, a Parisian living in Swansea; consequently, visits to the country increase in subsequent years.

My earliest solo visit to France is in 1964, a year when my annual leave is in September and I'm unable to find a companion who is free at that time. I take out a free pass through to southern Italy as that allows travel there by any route. In the event, France has an Indian summer and I go no further. In subsequent years, I visit every region of the country and develop firm favourites, among these, Provence and Alsace, my visits to these described in more detail in this chapter. Another favourite, the Massif Central is covered in *Exploring by train in France and Germany* (chap. 5) and Paris in one of *My favourite European capitals* (chap. 6).

There is so much I can write about this amazing country which attracts more visitors than any other in Europe. There are some great cities, among the best being Lyon; I first see this city at dawn on a July day in 1958, rubbing my eyes as the overnight train approaches the city, crossing the river Saône with the sun rising, just stunning! Josiane and I visit Lyon in 1999 and spend a few days there enjoying its historical centre and the superb food, for which it is highly rated.

Lille is a surprising city which I first see in 1964 when it looks down at heel; staying there early this century is a revelation as I see it totally transformed into a stylish modern metropolis. Bordeaux is another surprise, an elegant and graceful city with a fine historic core and a beautiful riverside location.

I present readers with an iconic image of Provence: azure blue window shutters.

Fréjus

Provence Alpes Côte d'Azur

To a 15 year old, my visit to Menton is electrifying and the start of what is to become a lifelong attraction to the Côte d'Azur. In the past 25 years, I discover more of this beautiful region as Josiane and I take holidays in each of two contrasting places, Nice and Fréjus, using them as a base to explore the region. Nice visits are generally off-season when its weather is more agreeable and Fréjus is usually June or September.

The Ligurian Coast

Right: the old town is a charming area of narrow streets, lots of people, washing hanging out between buildings. Its church and general backdrop looks distinctly Italian even up to the present day. In the foreground is the harbour, marina and beach. What a lovely place! (author)

Menton

My first visit to France in 1958 is to Menton on the Ligurian coast. *Liguria* was the ancient Roman province that spanned the eastern French Riviera and the western Italian Riviera. The place is an immediate hit, an Italianate town by the sparkling Mediterranean, with beautiful beaches and a fascinating old centre with narrow streets and buzzing with people. Very little of the old town has changed in sixty years and even the newer town and seafront remain as appealing as ever. In 1958 I stay in *Hotel Claridge's* near the station and from its first-floor dining room there is an excellent view of the railway; I'm thrilled as I see the procession of overnight trains from Paris at breakfast and returning to the capital at dinner time. All trains are hauled by Canadian-built steam locomotives (war reparations), robust and utilitarian oil-burning beasts; fascinating!

We spend lots of time on the beach and haggle with itinerant pedlars from North Africa plying with wares on their back, beating them down on price though rarely ending up buying! Drink is cheap and consumed in quantity by some, leading to high spirits in the evenings; I buy *Martini* because it's cheap though don't really like it. Food in the hotel is excellent and I develop a taste for massive tomatoes stuffed with herbs, also for peaches and apricots which are plentiful. We make two day trips; one is into Italy (Ventimiglia), the main purpose of which seems to be for us to buy cheap *vermouth* for the teachers to stay within their limits through customs. The other is to Monaco/Monte Carlo, an independent republic and to me, a surrealistic place where I see untold wealth on display.

I return to Menton occasionally in later years, stay one night in 1979, though not in *Hotel Claridge's* which has by this time become a dump! On my several stays in Nice earlier this century, Josiane and I make day visits there, notably in June 2008, fifty years on from my first visit. It's a place I never tire of.

Monte Carlo and Monaco

On our 2014 stay in Nice, we take a bus to Menton, an hours' highly scenic trip along the coast for just €1.50 each and en route, get a bird's eye view of Monaco. A day or two later, we take the same bus to Monte Carlo and look around this amazing city built into the hillside, covered in high rise buildings. A Monte Carlo 'must see' is its famous Casino and though we take a look around inside, see the fascinating arena where the gaming takes place, fight shy of trying to win our fortune, and decide to save our money. Along the road from the Casino, we find a tiny church beneath a bridge carrying the main road above the bay.

Monte Carlo is full of surprises, not least how all the tall buildings cling on to the hillsides. One could be forgiven for thinking that the city worships only money, so it's a surprise when we discover a tiny church tucked beneath a dual carriageway. It seems both God and Mammon are properly represented in this place after all!

Church, *left* and Casino, *right*

(author)

The independent Principality of Monaco has Monte Carlo within its boundaries and sits on a hill overlooking the bay, has a fine palace and a fascinating maze of streets. The bus fare for the one kilometre journey each way is €2, more expensive than the trip from Nice!

Left: the Royal Palace of Monaco sits on the hill above the bay and the city of Monte Carlo. It is the home and seat of Prince Albert II, reigning monarch of the Principality since 2005 having taken over from the well-known Rainier III.

The remainder of the area seems to be residential with some commercial activity. The real estate looks sumptuous (author)

Nice

Right: a magnificent view of the city from the Colline de Château (Castle Hill). The *Promenade des Anglais* runs for several kms along the coast; there is a permanent street market (centre left) and the old town is behind. Immediately below the hill is the very old quarter and the harbour (author)

Nice is at the western extremity of the ancient province of *Liguria*, and carried the name *Nizza* (still used on bilingual signs) though it is less Italian looking than Menton except in parts of its old town. My first visit is on a hot July day in the late 1980's and it is far too humid and noisy for my liking. Thus it stays off itineraries for a staying holiday until a happy accident of fate in late February 2002 when we decide to see the Fête des Citrons held in Menton and make Nice our base. We manage to get accommodation, with difficulty, at the *Hotel de la Fontaine* and find out why there's a problem; it's also the time of the *Carnaval de Nice* (Nice Carnival). This means we now see two colourful regional festivals and introduces us to Nice in the off season and realise what a pleasant city it is. At the eastern end of the *Promenade des Anglais* is the old town with its colourful market, narrow streets and shops selling a variety of traditional Provençal goods and souvenirs; don't we just love it! There are numerous very smart hotels along the Promenade, the most impressive being the *Negresco*, one of Nice's finest.

Left: the *Carnaval de Nice* is one of the most colourful displays we have ever seen and are so impressed we come back to see the same display two years later. Each year has a theme and the first time for us it is the introduction of the Euro and one float has John Bull in top hat flushing Euros down the loo! The Carnival moves along the famous *Promenade des Anglais* and our hotel is in the next block so it's a short walk. Here it is seen passing the famous *Negresco Hotel* (shutterstock)

We make several visits and in 2008, I discover that the railway line from Cannes to Grasse - the town famous for its perfumes - has reopened after being shut since the 1940's so we make a visit. The journey is not easy as our train breaks down just outside Nice and we have to wait for the next, missing our connection at Cannes, so we lunch there and arrive at Grasse in early afternoon. All ends well, we have a great day at the *Fragonard* factory learning how perfumes are made (and get some real surprises, including the cost of buying lots of small bottles for relatives back home!).

Left: much of Nice is very modern though there is a substantial part of the city that dates back to the 19th century. It is in two parts, here on level ground behind the promenade and street market where Josiane is enjoying window shopping at the many boutiques. Further east on the hill between the main city and harbour is a tightly packed area of narrow streets with fascinating shops and fine old buildings and is constantly busy with activity, and beyond that, a fine harbour and Marina. In all, a most agreeable city! (author)

Most of our trips to Nice are made by air, usually from Bristol, and we use local public transport which is convenient and cheap. There is a lot to do in the city, particularly in the old town, which is very colourful and bustling, with some great places to eat.

Getting around Nice becomes easier after 2004 with the introduction of a fine new tram network which transforms travel within the city. We also make excursions to Antibes and Cannes, the latter a particularly fine place and it's usually a local train trip though we use the bus once for the 1½ hour journey at a cost of just €1.50. The trains, though faster, are not very reliable which I think is a great shame as progress on congested roads is very slow. Another transport mode, a Land Train takes us to Castle Hill, a promontory where we get great views overlooking the city and the famous *Promenade des Anglais*.

Stylish modern trams serve the city including the airport (author)

The Var Region

Fréjus and St Raphael

My first visit at St Raphael is in 1996; it is the only place where we spend more than a two days in a two-week motoring trip with Josiane, starting and ending in Grenoble. It is a haven after previous stays in Barcelonette in the Provencal Alps which doesn't impress, followed by a 'distress purchase' at the *Ibis Cannes la Bocca*, a hotel desperately in need of a make-over; we get some compensating pleasure visiting the internationally famous Cannes *Carlton Hotel* and an hour in its sumptuous lounge for the price of two coffees!

St Raphael from the sea: a fine city with a backdrop of the Provence Alps (author)

We use our stay to visit several places round about, including a trip to see the steam train operations of the *Chemin de Fer Provence* narrow-gauge line between Nice and Digne through the Provençal Alps, a birthday treat from Josiane. We don't visit St Raphael's twin town of Fréjus which in retrospect is a pity as when we finally decide to give it a try in 2008, we are hooked.

In that year, we fly from Bristol to Marseille, a once-weekly service to what is a minority destination for tourists, even though it is France's second city. We rent a car and travel hopefully to Fréjus and finding accommodation at the *Hotel l'Arena (left)*, an instant hit; we've made the right choice and are to return on a further three occasions. Apart from being a great place in its own right, Fréjus is also a good centre for exploration, particularly towards the Alps and to the fabulous resorts along the coast to St Tropez. The town has ancient roots, being a key Roman fort and largest port on the Mediterranean. Its coastal strip, known as Fréjus-Plage, is very modern.

The old town hosts an open-air market on two days each week that is among the best in France and is held in the square next to the small but impressive cathedral of St Léonce. The adjacent streets spring to life with stalls selling all manner of goods. Josiane finds some very comfortable casual footwear and buys more on subsequent visits. Several times, we buy the excellent local terrine for picnics which we take in the surrounding countryside.

Above: the market at Fréjus; St Léonce cathedral in background

Right: a quiet street scene in Fréjus

Below: street art in Fréjus (all three by the author)

As well as to St Tropez and other coastal towns we head north and experience completely different countryside, very quiet with beautiful hill towns, though the roads are hazardous with narrow carriageways and deep cesses on either side, a danger especially when locals drive with such speed! The risks are well worth the effort and one of our favourites is Fayence, a town which always seems to be full of colour, and a string of fascinating adjacent hilltop villages. We sometimes stop for dinner on our way back at Bagnols-sur-Foret, another attractive village where we eat *al fresco* in the summer evening sun.

Back in Fréjus, the town is a delight of narrow streets, many decorated with artwork as this town has a well-known art school where students are encouraged to take their talents to the people; the surrounding lanes and narrow streets are sometimes festooned with colour and there are a number of craft shops. The nicest part of the town is the square around the cathedral, always busy even when the market is not there and as in so many such places, dotted with little cafes and larger restaurants where it is a pleasure to eat out on warm summer evenings. The town was originally one of the principal Roman settlements in the south and parts of its ancient walls and theatre are preserved. It is little wonder that we return to this place again and again.

St Tropez and Ste Maxime

The attractive harbour at St Tropez and the iconic church tower (author)

I have to confess to being sceptical that St Tropez, made famous by French icon *Brigitte Bardot* in the 1950's, would be other than a chic snazzy resort for the rich and famous so am pleased to be proved wrong. Our first arrival there is by boat from St Raphael, a journey of ninety minutes directly across the bay and a great way to arrive; this might seem long until it's done by road when takes an infinitely greater time due to chronic congestion!

Arriving at the harbour, there is a sense of relief as we find a charming resort which happens to have a flotilla of very expensive-looking yachts moored there. Behind this is an attractive town of narrow streets, with shops selling high quality goods, and a fine church with a most unusual looking tower. It is an expensive place to eat out but that is not unexpected. St Tropez has its own special delicacy, the *Tarte Tropézienne* which looks like a luxury custard slice though that would be doing the *Tarte* a disservice; its taste is exquisite, and it can be hard to get at times due to the high demand. Postage stamps seem to be difficult to get when I discover the local post office can't sell me any unless I sign a requisition which I think has to go through several layers of command for authorisation! Though it takes me another ten minutes, I seek out a *Tabac* and get stamps straight away.

Ste Maxime is an equally chic resort some kilometres north of St Tropez and is a much more modern town dedicated to the promotion of fine clothes, something Josiane is delighted with. It's attractive and expensive though in different ways to St Tropez and we thoroughly enjoy the place.

Left: nearby Grimaud is very attractive hill village not far from Ste Maxime though it's a devil to get into with its steep hills, hairpin bends, narrow streets and restricted parking; but we persevere and like it so much, go back several times. We find a superb restaurant with a beautiful veranda looking down over the distant bay and in the sunshine, enjoy some great lunches (author)

Strasbourg, Colmar and the Route des Vins

My first visit to Strasbourg is in October 1975, staying one night on returning from the Black Forest in Germany and I see the city only briefly in poor weather. I am to pass through in 2000 and 2001, both times on a through train between Germany and Paris after attending rail study tours. In 2002, with Josiane, I take a holiday here on a trip that also takes us into the Jura, the Black Forest and Colmar. We are so impressed with the city that we return again in 2013. Alsace and neighbouring Lorraine have a turbulent history with the region oscillating several times in recent centuries between French and German rule. Now firmly French, there are strong Germanic influences, not least in the local language of *Alsatian*.

Strasbourg

Prior to 2002, my impressions of this fine city are fleeting though is enough to convince me that a closer look is desirable. In that year, we travel using *Eurostar* and conventional *Rapide* train from Gare de l'Est in Paris (which just happens to be the *Orient Express*). We have booked an *Ibis* hotel opposite the station. I notice on arrival that the station entrance looks impressive in an amazing *avant garde* style which I see to greater effect from my hotel window. The ultra-modern tram network and the station entrance convince us that this medieval city quite happily blends its history with the present day. Our time in Strasbourg is split between three days at the start and two at the end with seven intervening days touring the Jura, west of Switzerland and part of the Black Forest.

Modern Strasbourg: tram (*above*) and train station (*right*)

On our third day in the city, we take a trip by boat to the site where the European Parliament sits and the European Court of Justice is located and again see some very modern architecture, though I don't find it attractive. In contrast to such modernity, we revel in the medieval half-timbered parts of the city, well pre-

served and maintained and visited by great numbers of people. Getting round the city is easy with a highly efficient and apparently trail-blazing tram network introduced some years previously by Strasbourg's first female mayor in the teeth of much opposition; her courage and foresight is completely vindicated as it's the easiest city to travel round in my experience.

On return a week later, we concentrate more on shopping and find a complete dinner service in *Provençal* style which is just what we've been looking for over some years in Provence! The vendor can't understand why we want to buy with him and pay for shipping it through a carrier but we are adamant. It still has pride of place at home on special occasions to this day!

Traditional Strasbourg: half-timbered *Petite France (author)*

Eleven years later and this time we arrive in Strasbourg by TGV; a connection from *Eurostar* at Lille, thence direct to Strasbourg over the newly-built *Ligne a Grande Vitesse de l'Est*. We stay for a week this time, and hire a car for three days for day trips to the *Route des Vins* and the Black Forest. First though, we make a much more thorough exploration of this extensive old city, its famous gothic cathedral of Notre Dame with its astrological clock, and the cluster of half-timbered buildings on the Grande Ile, many of which have fine restaurants. Alsace is a great place for eating and drinking and though I am a great fan of its wines, I cannot bring myself to like its most famous food dish, *Choucroute Garni* (Sauerkraut). What we can't do easily on foot, we do by tram and arm ourselves with all-day 'go anywhere' tickets each day we're in the city. This allows us to visit it's outer environs and the European quarter, where this time, we manage to get inside and see the Parliament chamber. By a quirk of the system at French insistence, one week's session per month is held here, so it is necessary for MEP's, civil servants and others to decamp lock, stock and barrel from Brussels twelve times a year. What this costs one can't imagine, but it's the EU and probably small change given its budget size.

We make the Black Forest the destination of a one-day trip; it isn't far away and we enjoy an idyllic day out, stopping first for coffee at the charming and scrupulously clean town of Oberkirch, afterwards taking a road through a heavily forested valley via Bad Peterstahl to the regional centre of Freudenstadt, a most attractive town where we have a fine German lunch; good, plain food well served with a light beer. The out and back journey on different routes is a part of the *Schwarzwald* I've not been to before and we revel in its outstanding scenic beauty. Our visit to Colmar and penultimate day tour of the *Route des Vins* is described below.

Right: Bad Peterstahl is the most attractive of a number of picturesque towns and villages on the road through the Black Forest (author)

Colmar and the Route des Vins

Colmar is a picturesque and interesting city to the south of Strasbourg with a small but significant medieval half-timbered sector. On our 2002 visit, we stay a night at the *Ibis* hotel outside the city on the way back from the Black Forest. We are relieved that the sun has come out after several days of rain and that the city is quiet in comparison to our previous night in Titisee, which turns out as the place where the cuckoo clock was invented and is full of shops displaying and selling them, with '*cuckoo*' sounds all day!

In 2013, we return to Colmar for the day by train from Strasbourg. I'm impressed with trains in Alsace, far more frequent than in other parts of France and we travel there on a Luxembourg-Basel through train.

Left: The old quarter of Colmar is grouped around and along the canal and the area is known as *Petite Venise* (Little Venice). It is a colourful and lively part of the city (author)

With more time to spend here than in 2002, we look around the busy city centre, then cross to *Petite Venise* where most of the half-timbered houses are to be found; this area gets its name from the small network of canals there. The city centre is of more recent vintage with many interesting buildings including a fine cathedral. Colmar is regarded as the centre of the *Route des Vins*, a string of picturesque villages situated in the Rhine Valley with its extensive vineyards.

We set aside two days to cover this area by car, starting at the north end near Strasbourg, where the agriculture is more mixed with fewer vineyards than further south. We visit the medieval town of Molsheim which we find fascinating, before heading south in the afternoon to visit Alsace's premier tourist attraction, the Chateau de Haut Koenigsbourg *(right)*. It has a very turbulent history dating from the Middle Ages to the early part of the 19th century when Kaiser Wilhelm of Germany has it restored as an historic monument. One can imagine how its role changed many times over the years, defending alternately French and German issues. It is busy with visitors and we confine ourselves to the grounds as the castle itself has too many steps.

The next day, we travel to the south end of the *Route des Vins* near Colmar, and progress north through a large number of very attractive half-timbered villages.

Left: At the area's principal area town of Barr, we stop to watch a troupe of dancers in traditional *Alsation* costume at its Foire aux Vins, a very colourful event held outside the Hotel de Ville. Such events add colour to an already very attractive series of 'chocolate box' villages along the *Route*. The half-timbered style is endemic throughout the area and all the settlements are surrounded by hills with vast areas of vineyards. The wine produced is very good.

Below: the square at Dambach, one of the larger villages on the *Route des Vins*

(author, both photographs)

It is interesting to see that the area almost totally given over to vineyards and villages serving these pop up every few kilometres along the route. It is a photographers' paradise. Our journey of discovery is over all too soon and at Strasbourg we celebrate with a glass of Alsace *Riesling* with dinner.

It's been a memorable week and it is with happy thoughts that we return to Lille on the direct TGV, connecting there to *Eurostar* to London and home to Swansea.

Auvergne and the Cévennes

This is a large part of rural France, unknown to many but for me it becomes a favourite, an area of outstanding scenic beauty with an interesting network of railways. Though I make some journeys there in the early 1970's, it is not until 1986 that I become aware of the vast area in the middle of France known as the *Massif Central* which includes the entire Auvergne Region and impressive Cévennes mountains.

Above: beautiful St Cirq Lapopie in the Lot Valley

Right: one of the places served by train 'TL' in the Haute-Loire Département is Le Puy-en-Velay. In this amazing place, iconic religious buildings are built on small *Puys* overlooking the town. It is on the section between St Georges d'Aurac on the *Cévennes Line* and St Etienne (author)

Travelling by train through this area requires skill in reading timetables, knowing the best places to stay and where to change trains. Largely remote and thinly populated, the railways reflect this with modest service levels and a network effect compromised by poorly co-ordinated timetables. I have travelled over 90% of the route mileage including lines that subsequently close; much of it has been in the ubiquitous Autorails, the X2800 *Massif Central* class built in the 1960's with powerful engines to tackle the severe grades.

Through the least populated areas of the *Massif* up until the late 1970's, train TL (Toulouse-Lyon) took a switchback course through Albi, Rodez, Mende and Le Puy. Although devoid of refreshment, the ten-hour journey was one of Europe's most interesting train rides. I manage to cover the whole route in stages at different times, though on train TL only once between Rodez and Le Puy. I enjoy the robust performance of the Autorail over the steeply graded Monastier-Mende-La Bastide route linking the *Causses* and *Cévennes*.

Much of the route has lost its passenger service, or has it severely curtailed and the only fully active lines are between Toulouse and Rodez; and Le Puy and Lyon. Schedules were much too slow to be competitive and the middle section is among the least densely populated areas of France.

The two north-south routes between Clermont Ferrand and the Mediterranean coast are thrilling rides. The *Cévennes Line* has for years had one train each way aimed at tourists as well as providing basic travel needs. Named the *Cévenol*, it starts out as a *Panoramique* Autorail from Vichy to Nîmes, upgrades to a *Corail*-equipped locomotive-hauled train between Paris and Marseille and has now reverted to a Clermont Ferrand to Nîmes railcar without any distinction. I travel the line in the locomotive-hauled era and a pleasant and exciting experience it is; with countless tunnels and viaducts, it traverses the spectacular Allier Gorges and at its south end, a fascinating post-industrial landscape.

Left: Grandly named La Bastide-St Laurent-les-Bains is the junction on the *Cévennes Line* for Mende. Its status in recent years has declined as through trains are introduced between Mende and Montpellier, both in the Languedoc-Roussillon Region. Here the northbound *Cévenol* (left foreground) arrives and the afternoon Mende Autorail connection waits (author)

Right: one of France's most amazing structures, the Viaduc de Garabit, designed by Eiffel, is on the *Ligne des Causses* south of St Flour. Despite its sparse service, the route is electrified, and in this photograph, the mid-morning Neussargues-Béziers train is crossing. At the time, it was one of only two daily return services (author)

The other line, aptly named *Route des Causses* (reflecting the high moorland it passes through) has a much bleaker time. When I first know of it, there are two trains between Béziers and Paris, one overnight and one daytime: *l'Aubrac*. Now it is just one regional daily train each way between Béziers and Neussargues. Electrified as part of the P.O. Midi investment early last century, its fall from grace has been hastened by construction of a fast *Autoroute* without corresponding marketing by SNCF for this *very* scenic route, which, throughout its length, is superlative, more so even than the *Cévennes* route.

Running transversely from Clermont Ferrand to Toulouse is another very scenic ride. A through route attempting to serve a number of non-contiguous markets and connecting with other trains at several nodes, its service is haphazard. En route are the attractive towns of Aurillac, Figeac, Villefranche-de-Rouergue and Gaillac and some amazingly beautiful villages such as Najac and Cordes-en-Ciel. It has only one daily through service, all others requiring changes and sometimes long waits.

Left: the Clermont Ferrand-Aurillac route skirts the southern edge of the *Puy* country. Puy Mary is one of the highest of the volcanic mountains in Cantal north of Aurillac (*shutterstock*)

Below right: the historic town of Villefranche de Rouergue is the main settlement between Figeac and Gaillac; like many French rural towns, it hosts a fine weekly market (author)

The principal connecting services are at Aurillac (for Brive), Capdenac (Brive-Rodez line); and Tessonnières (for Albi). All are on scenic rural lines serving attractive towns and villages. In my years of travelling, services remain static despite changing markets; the scenery doesn't change and I rate them as being in the top bracket of picturesque rides. These interesting routes, now operated by modern railcars, are crying out for improvements and marketing.

There are two lines serving the mountain town of Bort-les-Orgues and years before, an extension to Ussel was severed by construction of a dam. I have interesting experiences of both, first when staying at Riom-ès-Montagnes on the Bort-Neussargues line. In the evening, I wander down to the station as the southbound train arrives; only this one is the last ever! I'm surprised it has lasted this long considering Riom is the routes' only significant settlement.

Some years later, I travel with Peter on the other line to Bort from Aurillac; under notice of closure, its single railcar has a handful of passengers. It's a Saturday and on arrival at Bort, the connecting bus has gone; stupidly, I've read the Sunday timetable, when the connection is scheduled! We go into town for lunch, the restaurant owner has a taxi and offers to take us to Ussel. He does this with such speed and bravado, we wonder if we will arrive alive; however, we make our connection to Limoges!

Left: The small terminus at Le Mont-Dore where the locomotive for the *Thermal Express* to Paris is backing on to its three coaches. It will soon be struggling with the 1 in 22 grade to the junction at Laqueuille. In the platform is the Autorail which will stand idle all day while a bus covers the branch shuttle (author)

Another route still open but I suspect only just, has the steepest railway grade in France (1 in 22) from Le Mont-Dore to Laqueuille which for many years hosted the *Thermal Express* (Le Mont-Dore and La Bourboule are Spa towns). On a motoring holiday with Josiane in 1995, while she is at the local market in Mont-Dore, I take the train the 6 kms to the junction of Laqueuille. This portion of a through train to Paris starts out with just three carriages and its diesel locomotive has a struggle getting up the hill. On return I get an SNCF bus which I find odd as there is an Autorail and train crew parked all day at Mont-Dore; an example of the bizarre economics of SNCF, all too common, especially on rural lines. The Autorail operates morning and evening trips to Laqueuille but sits in the terminus during the day and a bus does the off-peak local trips. A bus is much cheaper to operate than a train (fact) but with an idle train and crew and the cost of a bus and driver, in practise it's actually more expensive (inconvenient truth)!

Finally, a brief mention of two routes to the small city of Rodez which has the distinction of being one of only three remaining termini for sleeping car service in France (the others being Albi and la Tour-de-Carol)! I have travelled on both routes and can vouch for what interesting journeys they are. The principal route is from Brive la Gaillarde, (on the Paris-Toulouse route) via Capdenac (where connection with the Clermont Ferrand-Toulouse route is made) and over some very demanding hilly terrain on to Rodez. The other route, shorter though busier, is from Toulouse to Rodez via the historic city of Albi with its massive *Cathar*-age cathedral. It also boasts France's second highest railway viaduct (viaduc de Viaur).

Left: the massive bulk of Albi Cathedral towers over the diminutive Toulouse to Rodez and Millau Autorail. The train service between Toulouse and Albi is quite frequent by SNCF standards and includes some loco-motive hauled trains for this is a commuter route, though it is very rural beyond Albi (author)

The Black Forest and Bavaria

My first experience of Germany is in 1970 when returning from Switzerland travelling most of the Rhine Valley from Basel to Köln. I then learn that Germany still has steam trains operating in some rural areas, which prompts visits to Bavaria and the Black Forest (*Schwarzwald*) in subsequent years; both areas are attractive for their scenic splendour and interesting rail networks. I get a thrill at Ulm in 1971 when I see a train from Friedrichshafen hauled by a 03 *Pacific*, just months before its withdrawal from service. Ulm is also noted for having the tallest cathedral spire in the World.

Above: Würzburg *(shutterstock)*

Right: the Wurzburg to Hof train ready to leave Bamberg under steam power (author)

A year later I am in Bavaria specifically to travel on routes known to be operated by *Pacifics* in their final years' service. My first solo journey to Germany has been interesting travelling via the Ruhr and a rural cross-country route between Hagen and Kassel. My Bavarian adventure starts in Würzburg, a historic university city surrounded by glorious countryside. In railway geography, Würzburg is where main lines to München and Passau divide with secondary lines north and south. That to the north interests me as one of the last outposts of steam operation still extant north of Bamberg.

The day starts foggy but by the time of my train, the mist has cleared and it's a perfect day. The train for Hof is electric-hauled to Bamberg where I get my first sight of German main line steam locomotives as two back on to my train, headed by the oldest in the fleet 001.008. It's a short train though the route is heavily graded and as I don't see any other trains double headed all day, as-

sume it's a positioning move for the second locomotive. The journey is through delightful countryside on the electrified line towards Halle in East Germany before diverging to the cross-country route to Hof at Lichtenfels. I alight at the large junction of Neunenmarkt-Wirsberg and spend time photographing its interesting railway scene. It is at the foot of the infamous *Schiefe Ebeine* incline, which my next train is about to tackle, hauled by a 03 class Pacific of younger vintage than the 01. With eight coaches, it's hard pressed and keeps good time on the sinuous route to Hof.

Hof is in West Germany (just) so I don't go through formalities as I'm returning south the next morning. I take a morning train from there bound for Stuttgart, retracing the route to Neuenmarkt, steam hauled by a 01 *Pacific*. After reversal, it is diesel hauled to Nürnburg via Bayreuth (birthplace of famous German composer *Wagner*). Arrival in Nürnburg is midday and I change for a cross country train to Stuttgart hoping to get to Tübingen that evening to see the last of Black Forest steam operation. I make

Above: a Nürnburg train leaving Hof in early evening (author)

Right: plenty of activity during my enforced wait in Ansbach (author)

an error by alighting at the junction of Ansbach and discover it is three hours to the next onward train. At least I get to see a procession of intercity and freight trains all afternoon. A late evening arrival at Stuttgart and no available accommodation sees my plans in ruins so I book a couchette overnight to Paris.

It is 1975 before my next short break in Germany, this time in the Black Forest and southern Bavaria. I am aware that steam traction ended two years ago but most main line trains are hauled by vintage diesel-hydraulic locomotives. My journey in the *Schwarzwald* starts at Offenburg in the Rhine Valley where I change to a regional train to Villingen. It traverses a magical landscape of mountains, forests, picturesque towns and villages and at Villingen, I change to a local train for the short journey to Rottweil. At Trossingen, the station is out of town and a little tram is waiting for the run to Trossingen Stadt, 5 kms distant. Rottweil, a key junction, is a delightful town even though its name conjures up images of fierce dogs. I stop for lunch before boarding a train (originating in Milan and bound for Stuttgart), to nearby Horb; these are notorious timekeepers, attributed to late handovers at the Italian border and this is no exception, running an hour late. It's a 35-minute journey on to Horb, an important junction on the *Schwarzwald* network.

I stay the night, giving plenty of time to explore this interesting town as well as observe its train operations. The main line goes north to Stuttgart and is the route of express trains; two local lines head north-east to the Tübingen and north-west to Freudenstadt, operated by the ubiquitous 4-wheel rail buses. Until a few years ago, it was a stronghold of the last Prussian-built steam locomotives class 38 and 78 and the newer class 64 on the Tübingen shuttle. The town of Horb is in a delightful setting perched on a hill surrounded by forest and has some colourful and decorative buildings.

A busy morning scene at Horb station, Stuttgart-Milan express and local railbuses (author)

I take a southbound Stuttgart to Milan train, which, as it is only an hour into its journey, leaves on time and is hauled by a diesel hydraulic locomotive. I am en route to Konstanz today but get off at Rottweil to explore this fascinating town which, like Horb, has a lot of colourful and decorative buildings though the impressive Rathaus (Town Hall) is covered in scaffolding.

The colourful main street of Rottweil in the Black Forest (author)

I leave at midday on an express train that takes the main route to Singen and terminates at Konstanz. This suits me as I wish to take the lake steamer along the Bodensee (Lake Constance). I have ninety minutes wait for my ferry connection allowing time to explore the town and the lake side. When I board the ship, I look back and see an old man playing a trumpet, amusingly accompanied by a duck in a bag, quacking (though not in harmony with the music!)

Konstanz is on a peninsula on the west of the lake and our steamer first crosses to the north shore to call at Meersburg; here they specialise in growing vines producing dry white wine, rare in a Germany more noted for its fruity *Reisling*. I meet a young lady from Canada on her gap year travelling on *Inter Rail* and we share a common interest in European travel. There are eight more stops including Friedrichshafen before arrival at Lindau, a journey of three hours which has been most pleasurable in the warm autumn sunshine.

Lindau is a popular quality tourist destination close to the Austrian border, but I find it's expensive to stay in though it is too late in the day to change my mind, so I pay up and enjoy a pleasant evening in the historic town. It is full of interesting buildings and is also an excellent railway centre; being close to the borders with Austria and Switzerland, it sees locomotives from German, Austrian and Swiss railways.

Left: the attractive town of Lindau on the shores of the Bodensee *(shutterstock)*

I leave Lindau on a train to Zürich and within ten minutes I'm on the border in Austria at Bregenz and a further fifteen minutes later, in Switzerland, opposite Lindau across the Bodensee.

I am to visit southern Bavaria again in 1992 with Robert; he has mapped out an utterly fascinating and highly scenic itinerary. We leave Innsbruck in Austria on a minor line to Garmisch-Partenkirchen in Bavaria, thence weaving in and out of Austria through Reutte-in-Tirol and a whole host of diesel-operated lines taking in Memmingen, Kempten and Oberstadt before arriving at Lindau again. Our journey continues through Bregenz and Buchs (Austria) to Chur (Switzerland) a truly international day's travel!

An interesting fact that Robert brings to light is that there is almost as much of the Tirol in Germany as in Austria. The railway scene here is fascinating and I see places that have hitherto been just names on a map, like Garmisch-Partenkirchen and Mittenwald.

Left: a colourful railway scene at Reutte-in-Tirol, Austria (author)

6 My favourite European capitals

Paris   Vienna   Prague

I write in other chapters of beautiful European cities such as Venice and Strasbourg. There are so many really fine, interesting cities in Europe that it's impossible to do them credit in this one book, so I have taken my 'top three' capitals: Paris, Vienna and Prague.

Paris has to take top billing as a city I have always loved since my first visit in 1959 though more importantly, it is where the love of my life comes from and consequently, I get to know it better than ever. What intrigues me about Paris is the wealth of interesting places and things to do off the beaten track, thus I concentrate a lot of my narrative on these aspects of the city. Added to this is that I have very few photographs of the main sites having visited them on my schools trip in 1959, *sans photos*. This photo is all I have of the Eiffel Tower, looking down from halfway up, as far as I get in recent years.

Left: Paris is at its best in Springtime, not too crowded and often with lovely weather. Here, I look down from the Eiffel Tower from the halfway point. The tower is of course almost constantly visible due to its height. I see it at its best on an evening in 2006 when we take our granddaughter to see the newly-activated and moving lighting display (author)

The other two cities, Vienna and Prague get more of the 'tourist' treatment as my time there is limited so I concentrate on the better-known attractions though in both cases stick to my mantra '*the traveller sees what he sees*'. Fortunately, both cities have many interesting sights off the main tourist trail.

I visit most other capital cities in Europe, and each has distinctive attractions. Madrid has its wonderful *Prado* Museum which takes a full day to see; Athens its historic Acropolis and Parthenon though it's too hot to appreciate these fully. Copenhagen has the world's finest entertainment park, the Tivoli Gardens and of course the famous *Little Mermaid*; and many more.

On my first visit with the school in 1959, our group goes for the big sights: the Eiffel Tower, Louvre, Notre-Dame and others so I see no need to replicate these in subsequent visits. However, many of my trips up to the early 1990's have tended to concentrate on the area on the Right Bank of the Seine and the Left Bank remains largely undiscovered. That is to change after 1993.

Josiane and I meet in that year and marry in 1995. For our honeymoon I suggest we go to Europe's most beautiful city and Josiane retorts that she doesn't wish to go to Paris; I actually mean Prague so have to retract and agree that it is number two after Paris in my European ranking.

Josiane's family lives in the *6th Arrondissement* on the Left Bank and I get to know this part of the city so intimately that it almost becomes a second home. For most visits, we stay in the *Hotel Terminus Orléans*, a friendly establishment near the major transport node of Porte d'Orléans where metro, trams and buses converge and connect. As a transport professional, I find it fascinating; in recent years it gains a tram route as traffic grows so much it outstrips the capacity of articulated buses.

Left: near to the Porte d'Orleans is the attractive shopping, café and restaurant hub of Alésia which is always bustling and has excellent fruit, vegetable, fish and meat markets and a great *fromagerie*. Overlooked by the impressive *St Pierre-de-Montrouge* church with its sonorous bells, it provides a lovely backdrop as we drink coffee mid-morning in the *Bouquet d'Alésia*. The whole area is lively most of the time and over the years we patronise many of the fine restaurants hereabouts (author)

We enjoy the district around the Rue de Sèvres where the proper *Bon Marché* department store, one of the most exclusive in Paris, is to be found. There is also a restaurant in the Rue Dupin once owned by Josiane's mother, who had the distinguished title of *Tante Madée* and a Michelin Star to her name. Amongst the celebrities that came there were ministers from the late President Jacques Chirac's government and she received a luxury box of chocolates from the President each Christmas.

We have some favourites on this side of the river, notable among them is the Jardin de Luxembourg overlooked by the *Sénat* where the French Government meets. The Gardens cover a large area and are popular as a recreational area for Parisians and visitors alike. There are areas for *Boules* (Pétanque) to be played, sailing of model boats on the lake or just walking and relaxing.

Though we visit many times, see no activity of note in the *Sénat*; either they are not in session or security is so tight we are unable to witness comings and goings. One presumes they *are* doing something there! We spend a lot of time around the Montparnasse area with a main line railway terminus of the same name, though it is better known for having the tallest building in the city, the Montpar-

Right: the Luxembourg provides donkey rides for young children and our granddaughter, Emilia *(left)* and her cousin Juliette *(right)* are seen enjoying their ride in the park (author)

nasse Tower, situated marginally outside the protected *Haussmann* conservation zone with its strict limits on the height of buildings. It has a fine shopping area buzzing with life, restaurants and cafés. We sometimes take time out on the other side of the river; the Boulevard des Champs-Elysées is a favourite of Josiane's for its smart shops and of course its main icon, the Arc de Triomphe. We usually get there on the bus; the service in Paris is very reliable and inexpensive.

Left: morning rush hour at the busy Porte d'Orleans; here trams, buses and metro interconnect. The T3 tram runs east-west at 4-6 minute intervals and about twenty city and regional bus routes converge here. Metro Line 4 originally terminated at the intersection but now extended one stop to Montrouge. The tram is a recent addition, replacing the peripheral bus PC2 which went from standard to articulated vehicles before demand outstripped capacity (author)

Right: the Luxembourg Gardens covers a huge area on the Left Bank. At its northern end is the Palais de Luxembourg which now houses the French Senate fronted by a large boating lake and recreation area. On fine days, the Gardens are extremely busy with people enjoying themselves. It is also a haven of tranquillity from the frenetic pace of the city (author)

Left: It was a great surprise for me to step off a number 20 bus in the spring of 1976 and find myself three centuries back in the Place des Vosges. The buildings are today unchanged except for extensive renovation and cleaning and I feel the loss of some of its character. In the same general area are a number of Paris' famous sites, the Palais Royal, the Bastille (site of the infamous prison, a key catalyst in bringing on the French Revolution of 1789) and it is quite close to the banks of the River Seine and its prolific artists scene (author)

Another iconic area is Montmartre with its white-domed cathedral and colourful Place du Tertre. Situated on a hill, it is reached by numerous steps or a funicular railway. For me, the *real* Montmartre is in the narrow streets below, with constant activity whether arty or people just going about their normal business. There are days on each visit when Josiane spends time with her mother and I take off on an excursion, sometimes out of the city, though often hopping on a bus and alighting at different neighbourhoods, all of which I find have unique characteristics. On one such trip, I notice a twinning sign at the suburb of Bagneux *Jumelée avec Port Talbot* (twinned with Port Talbot). I can't help feeling how people from this chic suburb might compare their highly industrialised twin!

On my second visit to Paris in 1964, I manage to stroll around the sights when not chasing steam trains and take some interesting photographs including this one below right which is among my all-time best.

Right: artist at work in 1964 on the Pont Neuf. His subject is the iconic *Panthèon*

Below: colourful Montmartre and Sacré Coeur in 2010

(both by author)

46

Whilst on the subject of these earlier times, it fascinates me just how ancient some of Paris transport is! It isn't just the buses; the Metro is also a museum piece on many lines. Things begin to change markedly after the mid 1960's and now I rate Paris public transport amongst the best I experience anywhere.

Left: I can't resist a photograph of Renault buses of the unique design pictured here and still operating in 1964, thirty years after they were built. Amazingly, some carry on running until 1971. This is seen at the entrance to the famous Tuileries Gardens. Josiane tells me that when she started work in Paris, this type of bus was her regular means to commute, riding the open back platform (author)

Right: as with the buses, so with many of the Metro lines in Paris in 1964, still using rolling stock built pre-war and painted in drab colours. The photograph shows a Metro on an elevated line (note the red-painted vehicle, first class!). By this time, Paris had already introduced it first rubber-tyred Metro trains, an experiment which stands the test of time but is ultimately unsuccessful due to costs (author)

Modern sculpture contrasts with the *Statsoper* (author)

Though I visit this fine city on several occasions, it is only on a 1971 trip with my parents, that I spend enough time to visit the main attractions. All is rectified on my most recent European holiday which is to Vienna where Josiane and I spend a week and visit many of the fine buildings, museums and palaces. One thing we wish for but don't see is the inside of the *Spanish Riding School* and that is one place visited on my 1971 holiday.

We stay at a modern hotel near the banks of the *Donaukanal* and hopes this is the Danube are dashed when we discover it was built as a service canal for bringing goods into the city. On our first day, we take a tram into the centre alighting at the *Statsoper* (State Opera House), a fine building. Outside is a man selling tickets for a musical recital at the nearby *Haus der Musik*; he is dressed in period costume and seems genuine. We find he speaks English and French perfectly though is from Albania and tells me parts of his native country are as picturesque as North Wales where it seems he has visited once. We buy tickets for the following evening's performance; the *Haus der Musik* is in a minor street and looks like anything but an opera house. It is a six-storey modern office style building and a glass exterior lift whisks us to the sixth floor where there is a small 'studio style' room seating about 150 people. It is fully subscribed and a a small ensemble includes a pianist, violinist, cello player and two singers. It is quite a remarkable scenario, a concert full of atmosphere and fine music and some historic commentary.

As far as seeing and experiencing Vienna, it's difficult to know where to start. One big advantage of this city is its public transport network: trams, buses and metro. The brightly painted red & white trams are being rapidly phased out in favour of functional and less aesthetically pleasing modern vehicles, though the latter have an advantage of being mobility friendly.

Right: Quiet back streets and secluded squares are a delightful feature of this city (author)

We still have quite a lot of walking as the circular 'centre' of the city is accessible mainly by metro and some bus routes. The main feature is Stephansplatz - and impressive St Stephens Cathedral - a very busy place. Leading away from here are the principal shopping streets in the city where many famous coffee houses are to be found; one of the oldest features of the city, they date back several hundred years. As well as taking coffee, we patronise what is known as an *Imbiss* a street stall selling *Wurst* (German sausage) which comes in many varieties and is very tasty. Exploring further, we come across quiet streets and squares with beautiful buildings and churches.

Sometimes, we simply get on to a tram and see where it goes, getting off when we see something interesting. On one journey, we discover the famous Schloss Belvedere, said to be Vienna's most important landmark; regrettably there isn't sufficient time to visit. After that is a square with a massive monument to the Russian Liberation. We spend time in the impressive Hofburg Palace which includes the famous *Spanish Riding School* though we can't get to see the live show. The Palace environs contain the National Library (a modern building in the midst of historical styles) and a range of museums.

Above: Stephansplatz (author)

Below: Hofburg Palace (author)

There is a building outside the city which is a must see; it needs two changes of tram and a short walk to the Schönbrunn Palace. It is well worth the effort though we arrive too late to do the main tour; however, the short tour is enough to fascinate and to see how life was lived in the time of Empress Maria Theresa in her ancestral home. The guided tour gives a huge insight into the turbulent times of her era and we reflect on how well the city has survived such insurgencies.

The Schönbrunn Palace covers a vast area ; this is a small part of the palace (author)

Left: I discover that the Danube doesn't flow through the centre of Vienna; a taxi driver provides the explanation. The original city was about a kilometre to the north and a new 'commercial' city grew up on the present site; a canal was constructed to serve it. I am keen to see the Danube and take a tram out in the evening (author)

Right: another famous landmark of Vienna is the giant Ferris Wheel in the Prater Park (made famous in the film *The Third Man*). Back in 1992 I actually took the ride on it but on our recent visit, get no further than Praterstern train Station, with the Wheel in the background (author)

Vienna is a place we could spend the whole week and still not cover everything of interest. However, on our recent trip, we take two days out to visit two other cities of interest. The first is Salzburg, a place that Josiane has visited but I haven't. It is a three-hour train journey and is well worth the effort as the scenery is fabulous; our outward journey is upstairs in a double deck train run by private company *Westrail.* Salzburg is an amazing, magical place, well known through its association with *The Sound of Music.* We concentrate on seeing the city centre and its fine buildings and atmosphere, returning in the evening on a *Railjet* train complete with a rare luxury these days, a dining car!

Left: a panoramic view of the city of Salzburg; the famous castle is in the background and the River Salzach in the foreground (author)

Our other excursion fulfils a desire to visit not only another city - Bratislava - but also another country, Slovakia. Once seen as the poor relation of Prague after the splitting up of Czechoslovakia, it shows little sign of this. It appears prosperous and is certainly very historic with a fine castle and cathedral, and it's directly on the Danube, unlike Vienna. We have a great lunch; the main item on the menu is unpronounceable but consists of a goulash style meat dish with dumplings; at the end of the day, we have coffee in a stylish bar alongside the Danube.

Right: Bratislava's fine cathedral occupies a prominent position above the river and the city and surrounded by a lively public space. Nearby is a warren of narrow streets reminiscent of the old city (author)

Both journeys and our trip from and to Vienna Airport give me a flavour of Austrian (and to a lesser extent, Slovakian) railways and impressions are generally favourable. Both countries operate Intercity service under the *Railjet* banner. In Austria such trains are push-pull seven car formations, locomotive-hauled. Where trains have two portions, two seven-car rakes and locomotives are coupled. Most of Austrian regional and local services are equipped with modern diesel or electric multiple-units.

Prague's Old Town Square is the iconic heart of the city *(shutterstock)*

My first arrival in Prague is in 1992 in less than auspicious circumstances. Travelling overnight from Berlin with Robert and David, we are subjected to a rare kind of torture. The train is through to Bucharest, capital of Romania and includes a Romanian Railway couchette coach in which we are allocated three berths. The sheets are dirty and the toilets verging on unusable. The attendant locks doors to adjacent cars and himself away, so on arrival at Prague our first call is to a hotel to wash and brush up, followed by a great breakfast. Emerging from the hotel, we see the beautiful baroque Old Town Square. We have only a morning to explore this wonderful city before continuing south on the train to Vienna and pack in a lot of sight-

seeing. I vow to come back some day and that opportunity arrives three years later as I marry Josiane and we choose Prague for our honeymoon.

In April 1995, we arrive there by air on *Lufthansa*, having changed at Frankfurt. Unlike my arrival in 1992, Josiane has more time to adjust to the incredible culture shock than I did. We have a comfortable hotel in the city centre though it's more expensive than expected. Everything in Prague except hotels and taxis is very cheap and we are to enjoy some fabulous food at modest prices. We pack a lot into the three days here and start with the city centre, followed by the riverside area then the old city and Prague Castle on the far side of the river. The Old Town Square is most iconic with its fascinating Astronomical Clock (*left*) one of its main features.

The old baroque city extends to the river, where there are twin towers on either side. The one on the Old

Town side is called the Powder Tower, originally used to store gunpowder. The Charles Bridge, named after Holy Roman Emperor, is the main river crossing and dates from the 16th century. On the Far side of the river is the Malá Strana, a very picturesque quarter of the city with a relaxed air about it, and the location of some very fine restaurants which we patronise. Above this is the New Town where there are more gems such as Prague Castle, St Vitus Cathedral and perhaps best of all, the strikingly beautiful Loretta Church. Getting around the city is easy

Above: the Powder Tower on the east bank of the River (author)

Right: The Malá Strana on the west bank is a delightful and tranquil area away from the hustle and bustle of the main city. It has some fine restaurants serving excellent local dishes and is a great place to spend the evening (author)

and inexpensive and we travel by metro or preferably tram as this gives good views of the city particularly the routes along the riverside. On one journey the tram is nearly full when we board and we sit a few rows apart. Josiane is behind an old gentleman who converses with her in French. When the woman sitting next to her leaves, I dart into the vacant seat whereupon he warns Josiane I'm making a pass at her. She tells him *'but he is my husband'* and there are roars of laughter! He is Czech and speaks fluent French.

Left: you never know who you might meet on Prague's extensive tram services. This route is very attractive running alongside the River Vltava. The city's public transport network is so good and cheap that there is no need to resort to taxis; nevertheless, we do one evening and find that one fare is higher than the cost of our three-day travel pass! (author)

After our taxi extortion, we don't use any more except on the journey to the airport bus terminal. The driver says he can take us all the way to the airport for a fixed price and takes us on a sightseeing route; he seems genuine and lives up to his word, showing us the residence of the Czech Republic's new President, Václav Havel on the way.

7   Sensational Spain

A journey through its finest regions and a peek at Portugal

The Iberian Peninsula has, for as long as I remember, been the destination of choice for British holiday makers seeking sun and heading for the Costas. The prospect of being with lots of British people, eating English food and spending time lazing on a beach doesn't appeal, so Spain is off the agenda until 1975 when my father and I decide to go and seek out the last steam trains in the country.

We see our steam trains though for both of us 'real Spain' is a revelation as we discover a land steeped in history with great mountain scenery, good food and friendly people. The country is still under the Franco dictatorship which in some ways is charming as it remains largely undeveloped and very bureaucratic, though not threatening. The trains are incredibly difficult to use and infrequent on most routes with customer service a foreign concept. We are amused to find an old-fashioned bell boy taking our cases in a Madrid hotel and there are other features we note from a past age. Portugal is avoided as there are still tales of insurrection (whether true or not) so we don't take the risk.

That trip is enough to persuade me to go back which I do again several times with Peter and Paul. It is with Josiane in the late 1990's that I share my fantastic experiences and we stay in a unique hotel chain, State run *Paradors* which provide great experiences in truly historic buildings. I get to see some of the Costas and find a hidden paradise in Cadaqués, away on a peninsula to the east of the Costa Brava.

I have chosen four Regions which appeal to me most: Castilla y León, Castilla-La Mancha, Extremadura and Andalucia with a brief look at Catalonia. Portugal makes it on the last page with the city of Porto.

Spain's most impressive Plaza Mayor is in Salamanca (author)

Castilla la Mancha

Ciudad Real

On my first visit to Spain with my father, Ciudad Real, south of Madrid, is our ultimate objective to see some of the last steam-operated passenger trains in the country. They are to be found on a long cross-country route to Badajoz in Extremadura, near the Portuguese border, a ten-hour journey on an all stations train! We take a short trip of under an hour to Puertollano and back, hauled by British-built steam locomotives.

The journey from Madrid to Ciudad Real is through the plains of La Mancha, dotted with farms and vineyards, with mountains around its perimeter. There is a curiosity of the Spanish railway system here; our train back to Madrid is a '*parliamentary*' through from Badajoz, mandated by government to provide low prices for the poor to travel.

Toledo

My first visit to Toledo is in 1989 with Paul. We spend just a night and morning, insufficient to appreciate this characterful and historic city famous for its production of knives and swords. It is so fascinating that I return in 1992 with Peter and Paul, staying two nights to ensure a full days' exploration. The city stands above a deep gorge in a fortified position and the hillside settlement is topped with a large garrison exemplifying its military status. The original entrance to the city is a narrow bridge with a large stone gate. A former capital of Spain, it's a UNESCO World Heritage site. Despite the heat we fill the day sightseeing. It is a journey of 90 minutes from Madrid by train and there is a great sense of arrival at its Moorish style station.

Above left: the original gateway to the city of Toledo   *Above right*: a panoramic view of this historic city

Top: Ciudad Real: the train from Madrid (right) connects to Badajoz (all photographs by the author)

Castilla y León

On my first visit to Spain, I am amazed to find how scenic and historic it is though I've merely scratched the surface. It takes a film in the late 1980's, *Monsignor Quixote*, about a priest going off the rails in Castile, to make me realise the existence of some of Spain's beautiful cities. In 1992, I visit Ávila, Salamanca and Segovia and could have done with more time.

I return in 1999 with Josiane and take a train from Madrid, staying in Ávila and Salamanca before exploring Extremadura and beyond. Travel from Madrid to Ávila is on one of Spain's unique and famous *Talgo* trains which leave from Principe Pio Station taking a circuitous mountain route. The journey is a great introduction to this region of Spain.

Madrid's Principe Pio station with *Talgo* for Avila on the left (author)

Ávila

On arrival at Ávila, we stay in its wonderful *Parador* for two nights. First impressions are amazing as we see a completely walled medieval city, impressive from the outside, containing priceless gems within its walls. It is the home of Saint Theresa, who is celebrated in a comprehensive trail around the city taking in the places associated with her work and achievements. She is a rebel Saint and this comes out clearly in the interpretation panels. We love this place, but the heat is too intense for us to contemplate visiting everything in order, so we pick and choose what we think are the best. The faithfully restored city walls are its greatest feature (they are wide enough for a game of *boules* which we saw under-

The amazing sight of the city walls of Ávila *(shutterstock)*

way). However, I cannot resist the contrast with Carcassonne in France, which is just as complete but far more commercialised.

Salamanca

Salamanca is a two-hour journey from Ávila and although I have visited this fine city before, I'm keen to show Josiane its delights. We stay in its *Parador*, a grand building across the river and get an excellent view of the city from there. The day is spent exploring this famous University seat with its twin cathedrals and many other historic buildings designed in the *Plateresque* architectural style and beautifully restored to their former glories. The Plaza Mayor in Salamanca (*see title page*) is probably the most impressive in Spain, trapezoidal in shape, a very lively part of the centre where whole families and visitors come out in the evenings to eat, drink and socialise. In contrast, I find the modern part of the city less attractive and note that this divide between old and new is prevalent in many cities.

Left: the old part of Salamanca is a treasure house of historic buildings including churches. Unusually, it has two cathedrals which came about when it was decided to replace the original with new build. Instead, they decided to keep it! (author)

Above: The 'new' cathedral in Salamanca; the towers of the original one seen in the left background. There is a rational explanation for the two cathedrals; the city suffered a massive fire in the 18th century and a new cathedral emerged from the rubble; however, the old one had survived major damage and was therefore refurbished and retained. The city is also famous for its learning; the 12th century founded University of Salamanca is claimed to be the oldest in Europe, though I think Bologna in Italy might challenge that! (author)

Segovia

Whereas Toledo became famous after the Roman occupation, Segovia *was* a Roman city and has many artefacts to testify to the claim. I visit in 1992 with and have a two night stay as there is much to see here, and some sights are on the extremities. There is a lot of Roman interest; indeed, the name *Segovia* has Roman lineage. Most dramatic is a stone-built aqueduct which almost encircles the city and leads in on a long route from near-by mountains supplying water to this day. It has a fine Gothic cathedral which stands on a promontory; and a little way outside, an impressive fortress-like structure, the *Alcazar* with a history stretching back 800 years and rebuilt following a fire in the late 19 th century. It has variously been a royal palace and residence and now houses a military museum.

Left: Segovia is a very photogenic city, dominated by three structures, all pictured here: the Cathedral, the *Alcazar* and the Roman Aqueduct. Considering it was built almost 2,000 years ago, the aqueduct's robust construction has allowed it to function as a water supply to the city to this day. The picture nicely encapsulates the magnificence of the city's attractions (author)

Below: the impressive *Alcazar* at Segovia; cathedral in background (author)

Seville

Above: St Mary's Cathedral in Seville (author)

Right: Alta Velocidad Española trains at Sevilla *Santa Justa* (author)

It is 1989 when I first visit Seville, arriving in the Moorish style *Plaza des Armas* station and it is *very* hot. Lunch is taken *al fresco* in a city street which is covered by canvas sheets between buildings to moderate the intense heat. It is a nice meal interrupted by street vendors selling roses. Ten years later, with Josiane, I arrive in Seville from Antequera, find our hotel has nowhere to hand for parking, so I drop the luggage and return the car to *Avis*. Walking back to the hotel is through lots of narrow and picturesque streets and the hotel itself is an absolute gem with a centre courtyard and fountain, marble tiled floors, and oozes quality. After an excellent breakfast, we get out to the city early to avoid the heat which is just as well as by mid-day it is almost unbearable. The city centre is utterly fascinating with the Gothic Cathedral as centrepiece, full of people and very lively. It has lived through many very different eras from Roman through Moorish and Castilian and it is this historical diversity that is seen through the buildings and general air of this colourful place. In

the evening, we eat out at a restaurant with a *Flamenco* floor show and next day travel on the AVE high-speed train, from a striking new *Santa Justa* station The AVE was introduced in 1992 when a major international Expo was held in the city and the high-speed line was built in six years from conception in 1986. A train arriving more than five minutes late entitles passengers to a complete refund of fare; our schedule is kept to the minute so no refund for us! One feature of these trains marking them out from other European high-speed systems is the superior on-board service which even Josiane has to admit is well ahead of the French TGV.

Antequera

We have travelled south from Extremadura and cross the boundary into Andalucia where the land becomes flatter and the roads busier, and reach Antequera, an oasis of calm. It is a beautiful city and its *Parador* turns out to be a modern custom-built building and is none the worse for that. For a place neither of us has heard of before, we find there is a lot to do and see, a partly walled city with a much history within those walls. We have afternoon tea in a small café and for a refreshing drink, both opt for tea. Our waiter is clearly stumped as to how to make tea properly, so we help him: *warm the pot, pour absolutely boiling water in over the teabag and add milk after*. He makes notes and is delighted that he now knows how to do 'proper tea' so we compliment him.

Above: the castle stands sentinel over the city of Antequera (author)

Right: the one that got away; the modern regional trains in Spain (*on right*) look very nice and it's a shame we can't travel as they're so popular! The trains at Antequera travel a long cross-country route between Seville and Almeria via Granada (author)

It is said the best battle plans rarely survive first contact with the enemy: thus ours to take the train to Granada are thwarted by a reservation only train that is fully booked. The ticket clerk, clearly a product of charm school says just '*completo*' and slams the blind down; so we drive.

We spend a second night in the *Parador* and plan to travel to Seville the following day. I have mapped out a route via Malaga, Torremolinos and Ronda which will take us along part of the Costa del Sol and the incredible city of Ronda, built above a very deep gorge. We drive down to Malaga and, hoping to stop for lunch, find it is extremely busy with traffic and parking problems. Regrettably, we abandon our plans and return to Antequera reaching Seville by taking the direct road from there.

Granada

The Fortress and Courtyard of the Myrtles in the fabulous Alhambra Palace (author)

The road from Antequera is of motorway standard and it takes not much more time to get there than it does to find parking in Granada! The parking hassle is soon forgotten once we see the Alhambra.

Its beauty is difficult to describe in words but the Moorish style interior décor is quite new to us and the profusion of greenery and water makes the whole such an outstanding place. The Alhambra dates back to the 14th century when the Moors ruled Spain. The main building is the principal one of a number of palaces built on the site, the remains of which are visible. The intricate mosaics, sculptures and decoration are of a kind we have rarely seen before and credit must be given to the talents of those who designed and built this beautiful place. It occupies a commanding position in an otherwise largely unremarkable city. There is enough to see for us to spend the whole day here.

The return journey is broken by calling in at a motorway service station, not normally the most exciting of places but this one interests us. In the main restaurant is an elliptical bar with stools around and huge *Iberico Hams* hanging on hooks around the perimeter. As we wonder if many are sold, a local man comes to the bar, chooses and pays for one and walks out with his trophy, all in the space of five minutes; we have our answer! The service station has better food and drink than we are used to at similar places back home.

Extremadura is by far the most lightly populated region of Spain and is almost entirely rural. It is an utterly fascinating region with great scenery and history.

Ciudad Rodrigo

My introduction to this city is accidental. In 1989, Paul and I have a difficult time getting around by train due to strike action and our trip from Salamanca to Lisbon is cut short when the train terminates at Ciudad Rodrigo, a fascinating small city with a fine castle. The place is short of available accommodation and we have to settle on the castle which is a *Parador*, a state-run hotel, one of many throughout Spain introduced in the 1930's to rejuvenate deprived communities. The price is reasonable and we have our first night in a real castle, in a converted cell with thick walls and sumptuous comfort. Our room has a magnificent view looking out over the plain towards Portugal.

Guadalupe

A change of plan due to bad weather brings my friends and I from northern Spain to seek the sun. Thus we stumble on one of the most beautiful and remote small towns in Spain which again has a *Parador*, a converted hospital for pilgrims adjacent to its famous monastery. It is a near perfect location, surrounded by mountains and olive groves and far from anywhere else of note. There must have been a railway there many years ago judging by the impressive viaduct, its width suggesting narrow-gauge but from where and for what?

Top: the *Parador* at Ciudad Rodrigo, a medieval castle (author)

Above: Guadalupe with Monastery and *Parador* (*left*), disused viaduct (*right*). Its *Parador* is one of the finest in Spain and this remote town sits among the mountains and large areas of olive plantations (author)

Trujillo

Such is its remoteness that it is an 80 kms road journey west from Guadelupe to the next town of any size, Trujillo. This is a really thrilling place, once home of famous (or should I say infamous) conquistador *Francisco Pizarro* who is honoured by a statue of him on horseback in the Plaza Mayor.

Trujillo occupies a commanding position above the plains (author)

Trujillo is on a rocky hill overlooking wild heathland and distant mountains and is another impregnable fortress town. This and other towns in Extremadura were the birthplaces of most of the conquistadores and one wonders how men from such a quiet country region could inflict so much pain and suffering on the South American people.

Mérida

It is another 90 kms drive from Trujillo to Mérida, one of the largest towns in the Region with a history going back to Roman times; indeed, it is said that Mérida has more Roman ruins than Rome itself and I can almost believe it! This town was once capital of the Roman province of *Lusitania* and much of the old town, including the theatre, circus, bridge and aqueducts are sensitively preserved though the main town is quite modern.

There is much more to this province which I earlier travel through by train en route from Cáceres to Seville (the only one of the day, which demonstrates how rural this area is). I also return to Guadalupe and its *Parador* on a motoring holiday with Josiane in 1999.

Left: the well kept ruins of the Roman Theatre in Mérida which has been nominated the best preserved Roman building in the World (author)

63

A holiday that starts in Toulouse and takes in Barcelona nears its end as we find the secluded resort of Cadaqués east of the Costa Dorada at the end of a wild peninsula; it is one of the most beautiful places we have ever seen. Down by the bay, we book in at the *Hotel La Residencia* where our room overlooks the square and harbour beyond. An interesting fact is that it was a one-time base for *Salvador Dali*, the Spanish surrealist artist who stayed here prior to buying a house in nearby Port Lligat; we wonder whether he stayed in our room with its balcony view of the bay. Wherever we look is an overwhelming sense of colour and light; buildings with doors and shutters painted brilliant blue. Santa Maria church is beautiful outside and sumptuous inside with its gold leaf chancel.

Left: children with their granny off to the seafront (author)

Right: the town is in an idyllic setting around a wide bay. The water is very blue and is reflected in the lavish use of blue (deeper than the Provençal style) on doors and window shutters throughout the town. The church stands in a prominent position above the bay. It is little wonder that Salvador Dali adopts this place for his artistic inspiration! (author)

We are so impressed with this place that we return two years later flying into Montpellier and combine our visit with another look at the French western Mediterranean coast and a visit to the historic Catalan city of Girona. The visit allows us time to visit the Santa Maria church in Cadaqués which has a magnificent golden baroque altar piece *(left)* which is among the finest in Spain.

Portugal's second city : Porto

Porto is yet another happy accident for me and my friends. We have been motoring in northern Spain, and a combination of bad weather and poor roads leads to fatigue, so we leave the car at Tué in Galicia and take the train to Porto. We drive the short distance to border station Valença de Minho, park in Spain and

cross the border on foot, unchallenged, joining one of the thrice daily diesel railcars that run from Vigo to Porto. It's an interesting journey along the attractive west coast and we arrive at the amazing gem of the São Bento terminus in the city, beautifully decked in blue picture tiles, so typical of this country's buildings. The station is the prelude to an incredible city, perched precipitately on both banks of the River Douro.

Above: the famous view of the *Eiffel*-designed viaduct at Porto

Right: a lively street scene in Porto; note the highly decorative church

Below: neighbourhood watch (all photographs by the author)

All along the banks of the river are vintage barges and huge signs advertising different brands of Port wine which is what this city is famous for. The gorge is spanned by a magnificent *Eiffel* designed bridge. At lunch we ask for a glass of port to accompany our food and it takes a while for the waiter to find some; maybe the drink is just for the English and not much favoured in its home city. We soak up the unique atmosphere of this much under-rated city which has numerous historic buildings, many clad in decorative blue tiling. The transport system includes a trolleybus

network (with some ex-London vehicles) and a vintage tram line. Returning to the station through a maze of narrow streets, I feel I am being watched by one of its residents and can't resist taking a picture of the spectator! Before taking the train north, there is ample time to look around the amazing São Bento station, which, in addition to its fine concourse and buildings, has vintage signalling and rolling stock, a station of great character.

8   Iconic Italy

Venice, Florence, Bologna and Sicily

My first brief contact with Italy is in 1958 on my school outing to Menton in France when all participants make a day trip to Ventimiglia; it excites as a new experience though I am not too impressed with the place. It is to be another 13 years before I set foot in that country as part of a family holiday that has included Austria and Switzerland before staying in Lecco on Lake Como; and in 1977 on a journey with Paul, taking in Italy, Greece, Yugoslavia and Hungary.

The first year for me to spend significant time in the country is 1987 when Paul, Peter and I make Bologna a base for three consecutive day trips to Florence, Venice and Verona. Peter and I take a short break in 1991 to the Lake Garda region of northern Italy.

So my visits to Italy up to then have been fairly brief and it's not a country I've taken to my heart like France and Spain. This is to change following my marriage to Josiane; she loves the country and we have several holidays there in more recent years with some great experiences. I have chosen four places which most appeal to me; Venice, Florence, Bologna and the island of Sicily.

Getting around Italy by train has been relatively easy, certainly inexpensive and sometimes chaotic. Things get better in the present century as new high-speed railways (years in planning and execution) come on stream. On our visit to Bologna in 2016, we arrive from Milan on an Italian Railways (FS) *Frecciarossa* high speed train which I find most impressive. This is having strong competition from private operator NTV who operate similar 300kph high-speed services and we use one of them on a day trip from Bologna to Florence. I find it slightly inferior to the FS trains (Chap. 10).

The historic piazza at Ragusa Ibla, Sicily (author)

The Council Hall and Campanile (author)

My first visit to this beautiful city in 1987 is a brief one which makes an immediate impact and more than fulfils my expectations. With just one long day out, with Paul and Peter, we pack in a huge amount but merely scratch the surface. A return visit is made in 2008 with Josiane and we spend the first four days of a ten-day Italian holiday, staying in the suburb of Mestre. We visit the city on two of the four days (on the intermediate day visiting Verona) and on the first, take advantage of a free bus from the hotel which drops us close to the Grand Canal. Josiane is just as enchanted with her first view as I was eleven years earlier. We start with a light breakfast and purchase a public transit ticket with un-limited access to the amazing *vaporetto* water buses, an excellent way to see the city as we get on and off at will. First stop is the Rialto Bridge, then St Mark's Square which is so full of interest that it occupies a full couple of hours just visiting the Doges Palace.

A classic view of the Grand Canal showing the tremendous activity on this busy waterway (author)

We slip across the water to San Giorgio Maggiore and lunch in a small café, a one-man place where service is very rapid indeed for the large number of customers in the short intervals between *vaporettos* arriving; a brilliant lesson in time and motion study! We take a long trip on the water bus to get a feel for what more there is to see on our return next day and end the day in a restaurant alongside the Grand Canal. The next day sees us doing some exploration in the byways and a discovery that we can get a gondola for €1 a head (though just to cross the canal!) We visit more fabulous places and end the day at the *Arsenale*, the historic armaments depot which was utilised by the Venetian adventurers of old. It's been two fantastic days here and we move on to Florence.

Above: a view of St Mark's Square and Campanile from San Giorgio Maggiore. Note the gondolas laid up awaiting customers; not us though (author)

Left: one of the most iconic aspects of Venice is the Gondoliers. We enquire about hiring a gondola and are put off by the price. No matter, we spot one of the cross-water ferries operated by small gondolas and the gondolier is dressed in black strip tunic, so we pay our one euro per ticket and get an authentic looking trip! Here, Josiane (*lower left in picture*) and I enjoy five minutes of sheer bliss! (author)

My first visit to this city is in 1987 on a day trip from Bologna. First impressions are marred by traffic, pollution and heavy downpours of rain but I vow to come back one day. It is in 2008 and is the second city Josiane and I stay in on our ten-day visit. The *Hotel Londra* proves an excellent choice as our base and I'm pleased to find the city has cleaned up its act; less traffic, little pollution and sights to die for. We are advised to book in advance for the main attractions which we do for the *Duomo* and *Uffizi Museum*. At the *Duomo*, we enter by the wrong door for the main building, finding too late that it's the queue for the tower and 200 steps! It is really hard work but we both manage to climb most of the way and earn an ovation from the other visitors for our efforts! Josiane gets as far as 'hell' and I manage to climb 50 more steps to where 'heaven' is depicted inside the dome. It is easier coming down and we see the main part of the cathedral. The *Uffizi* is fascinating and it takes us a large part of the next day to see all its wonderful paintings and sculptures.

Left: the *Duomo*, Florence's most iconic landmark. Like most of the top landmarks in the city, we make prior booking to reduce queuing

Below: the attractive Arno riverside in Florence (both: author)

The unique *Ponte Vecchio* with its buildings on the bridge (author)

There is so much to see in this city, full of churches and other historic buildings and of course famous statues by Renaissance artists and sculptors. The *Ponte Vecchio* intrigues us, not only with its houses perched precariously over the river but on the inside, an almost complete monopolisation by jewellery sellers at prices that make our eyes water. A riverside walk completes a great day out.

We also take a day trip to Siena, a place I've heard so much and about and long wanted to visit, and there is a frequent train service taking two hours from Florence. We discover a really historic and attractive city in the centre of the Tuscany region; a treasure of history and general interest and the journey is a surprise as I hadn't previously realised how beautiful the Tuscan countryside is.

Left: this beautiful fountain is one of the best features of the fabulous Piazza Il Campo, a large open space in the centre of Siena flanked by an impressive Campanile on its opposite side. The rest of this city centre is typified by renaissance architecture and it has a lively feel about it. The journey there introduces us to the sheer beauty of upland Tuscany, popular with the British for second homes and I'm not surprised (author)

Bologna

When I stay here in 1987, it is as a convenient node for day trips to Venice, Florence and Verona and I miss out on the incredibly interesting place it is. It is many years later when Josiane and I come for a five-day break having been attracted by *Rick Steins'* TV series on great foodie weekends; it lives up to our expectations and more. We find a lively city with a strong commercial ethic as well as the oldest seat of learning in Italy. Its towers are the remnants of a whole host of them in medieval times, the height denoting the wealth of the owner. It is the crossroads of northern Italy. We discover that here one doesn't ask for *Spaghetti Bolognese*; the real thing is *Tagliatelle al Ragú,* one of the city's top specialities. It is close to Parma, world famous for its cheeses and hams, so we make a visit to that historic city (which has strong ethnic connections with Swansea).

Left: few (of the more than a hundred towers of medieval times) survive up to the present day though this one is the tallest in the city. We don't climb as there are only steps so instead, we get our panoramic view of the city by taking a sightseeing bus to the hills south of the city

Below: our panoramic view of the city showing just four towers extant, including the tallest (both photographs by the author)

For our 20th wedding anniversary, Josiane and I decide to go to Sicily after seeing the Italian TV drama *Inspector Montalbano*. Researching online, we discover that filming is done in several World Heritage towns there and we stay a week in Ragusa (fictional *Vigata*) at the *Antica Badia Relais* Hotel, a grand 18th century villa opposite the cathedral. We use this as a base to explore other places shown in the drama and it is so exciting with a wealth of beauty, culture and history.

It is no understatement to say that we are blown away by the most amazing heritage and beauty of both the cities and the landscape in which they sit. It is intensely disappointing to me in particular not to be able to travel on the incredible local railway though I see its spectacular engineering round about. I try without success to find out train times and where they go, so we travel round by car. The local buses are poor and the scruffy printed timetable doesn't correspond with information at bus stops; we do manage a couple of journeys on the minibus to Ragusa Ibla which saves us negotiating the hair-raising bends and chronic shortage of parking.

Ragusa

We arrive in Ragusa late in the evening after an 80 kms journey from Catania airport. The hotel is an excellent choice and as it is in the centre, good for exploring this fascinating place. There are two towns separated by a deep valley; the other is Ragusa Ibla, a perfectly preserved hilltop settlement full of historic buildings. Ragusa itself is a working town of 70,000 people and has a quite modern shopping streets cheek by jowl with a grid of older narrow streets and a sprinkling of historic places including the cathedral, various churches and civic buildings. In the lower part of the town there is great excitement when we come across a filming session and see the principal *Montalbano* characters, though we are not allowed to take photographs. There is a very smart shopping centre close to the hotel and we find the quality and (high) prices surprising in what we think of as a poor country. It seems tourism is relatively undeveloped, and the detective drama has been a catalyst for growth as we find out from talking to other visitors and locals.

Left: the Church of *Ecce Homo* (behold the man) in Ragusa. This is at the head of a street of the same name. The area around is formed of 19th century blocks, originally complete mansions converted to cheap dwellings; none of them have back entrances as they are part of a solid block. There are no parking spaces, hence use of the pavement (author)

There is a deep valley between Ragusa and Ibla which is traversed either by a very steep triple hairpin bend road or 340 steps down from Santa Maria delle Scale (*scale*: steps); not a great choice when making the journey!

At the bottom of the hill is La Chiesa delle Anime Sante del Purgatorio where people were presumably purged of their sins before entering sacred Ibla. The whole area around here is fascinating and historic and appears in a lot of *Montalbano* scenes. There are great views upwards in both directions to Ragusa and Ibla where we see an amazing landscape of historic buildings. There is another long climb - though with fewer hairpin bends - to Ibla. We do the trip on a minibus shuttle which overcomes the chronic shortage of parking. Ibla is sumptuous, breath taking and well worth the effort of getting there.

Above: The Chiesa de Santa Maria delle Scale (church of St Maria of the steps) is at the top of the hill in Ragusa and is sometimes seen in episodes of *Montalbano*. There are 340 steps to the floor of the valley (author)

Below: In the valley between Ragusa and Ibla where the Chiesa delle Anime Sante del Purgatorio is right of centre and the Chiesa Santa Maria dell'Itria is at left foreground. The photo is taken from the top of the steps and behind the camera is the twin town of Ragusa Ibla (author)

Punta Secca

One might assume from the *Montalbano* series that his home is in Ragusa though it is actually 30 kms away in the gorgeous seaside village of Punta Secca, exemplified by the lighthouse which appears in the series' opening shots. His house, when not used for filming, is let out as a holiday home, *Casa Montalbano*, and is booked up years ahead! The bay here is beautiful, typical of the pristine Sicilian coast. There is no sign of occupation or filming at the time of our visit.

Above: the iconic lighthouse, which appears in the opening sequences of *Inspector Montalbano*, is in Punta Secca

Right: the shoreline, again often seen in filming with *Montabano's* residence, the building with the attractive verandah, left of the tower. We are unable to gain access to the this as it is evidently in use

Below: the Basilica San Giorgio in Modica

(all photographs by the author)

Modica

Modica, about 10 kms south of Ragusa is recognisable from the *Montalbano* series as many scenes are shot in its very narrow streets which hug the hillside. Parking proves to be difficult but I persevere and find a less than ideal (and legal) spot to hurriedly take this, the Duomo di San Giorgio and other photographs of this incredible place. The old town is, like Ragusa Ibla, almost completely made up of heritage buildings with narrow streets.

Donnafugata

Another place we visit is the castle at Donnafugata which is the fictional   headquarters of Mafia boss *Balduccio Sinagra* and we look over the courtyard and balcony where a historic meeting was held between *Montalbano* and *Sinagra* to get key information on a rival Mafia gang!

Wine postscript:

I'm a lover of good wine and in Sicily, find my wine Paradise. Their white wines have a beautiful soft and mellow taste and I'm thrilled to find them now widely available in the UK.

Narrow gauge railway lines as normal commercial enterprises in Europe are now mostly modern networks. In the early years of railway building, they were the answer to more economical operation in lightly trafficked or difficult topographical terrain. Every European country, even as late as the 1950's had narrow-gauge branch lines, most on their last legs and disappearing fast. By the late 1960's there were just a handful in operation in western Europe though we were to discover a large number remained behind the 'iron curtain' which came to light, particularly in former East Germany, in the early 1990's.

In Switzerland in particular, many networks were constructed as metre-gauge and remain so to this day, having been subsumed into the national railway system as successful enterprises.

Many minor narrow-gauge lines survived in a sufficiently good state that they could be revived by railway preservation groups and these sprung up all over Europe, many becoming successful tourist attractions.

I travel on a number of these lines and describe in detail one each in France, Germany, Switzerland and Sweden, but, for reasons of space, have to leave out some very interesting ones such as the *Ligne de Cerdagne* in the French Pyrenees so here is a photograph to delight the reader.

The *Ligne de Cerdagne*, better known as *Le Petite Train Jaune* (the Little Yellow Train), is a 63 kms line in the French Pyrenees linking La Tour-de-Carol and Villefranche-le-Conflent. Electrified on the 'third-rail' system, it is over 100 years old, its local transport role is gone and is now a tourist attraction. It reaches a height of 1593 metres, has 19 tunnels and, surprisingly, just two bridges

A hard climb for the train up the valley of the Doux (author)

In September 1968, I visit this amazing narrow-gauge system with my father a few weeks before complete closure and experience it whilst still operational. A special train has been arranged and we join the tour at Lyon Perrache station for an early start on a local train. We expect an Autorail for the short journey down the west bank of the Rhône to Tournon; happily, SNCF has turned out a steam locomotive and rake of 6-wheel coaches for the train which of course delights us. Except for the guard; he is jumping up and down at a water stop as everyone wanders over the tracks taking photographs. Clearly unused to this bizarre sight, he mutters 'merde' and sits on the track with his head in his hands!

On arrival in Tournon we see our special which has to await arrival of a scheduled incoming railcar. The train is formed of eight vintage carriages and hauled by a powerful *Mallet* 0-6-6-0 articulated tank locomotive 403. It leaves the station on mixed-gauge track for 1 km north before turning into the valley of the Doux (*gentle* in English) though there is nothing gentle about this journey with severe grades, sinuous curves, tunnels and viaducts. It is nearly the end of the line for this once extensive narrow-gauge system in one of the most scenically attractive parts of France. Our steam train is a one-off and all regular services are run by railcars, due to end for ever in a few days. The carriages are festooned with the words 'NON A LA SUPPRESSION', a last ditch and futile attempt by locals to prevent closure. The train stops to take water in the small village of Boucieu-le-Roi where there is plenty of time to roam around.

From here on, it is an even steeper climb into the high country of the Ardèche and the next stop is Lamastre, one of the area's principal towns which has a reputation as the gourmet capital of France. There is a lengthy wait for another local railcar service to come and go.

Water stop at Boucieu-le-Roi (author)

From Lamastre, the line veers south-west and passes over a watershed and we get our first distant view of the *Puys* (volcanic outcrops) before dropping down to Le Cheylard, principal centre for the network from where branches lead to La Voulte sur Loire and Dunières, the latter to which our train is to head later.

The train stops at Le Cheylard for two hours where the locomotive is serviced and passengers can take lunch in the idyllic surroundings of this rustic French village. We buy filled baguettes and wine and sit on a stone wall in the sunshine watching the world move ever so slowly around us: it's perfect! There is a locomotive shed, sidings and workshop as it is the operations centre for the *Vivarais* system.

They tell us the best part is to come and after what we've already seen, it surely cannot be bettered; but it is! From Le Cheylard to the mountain resort of St Agrève (*Belvédère des Cévennes* as it says in the advertising), we have the toughest climb of the trip so far and a panoramic view of an immense volcanic landscape far to the west. From St Agrève, it is downhill to the terminus at Dunières where we connect into an SNCF standard gauge train. A diesel locomotive with a rake of 6-wheel coaches is waiting to take us to St Etienne. It is soon to be a very different journey as we enter an industrial landscape when it joins the main line from Le Puy at Firminy (limit of the PLM 1500v DC electrification). It trundles down the heavily industrialised valley to St Etienne, where our journey ends.

Le Cheylard, headquarters of the Vivarais (author)

Part of the *Vivarais*, from Tournon to Lamastre was restored a year later and, apart from a break from 2008 to 2013 has operated every year since.

Left: a Harzquerbahn train bound for The Brocken departing Wernigerode in early afternoon. It is to face the steepest climb of the network out of here, mostly at 1 in 30 to Drei Annen Hohne; the rest of the line to the Brocken is only slightly less steep. The Brocken (1,141 metres) remains the most popular destination to this day (author)

It is two years after re-unification of Germany when I first visit the remarkable 100% steam-operated Harzquerbahn narrow-gauge system. With Robert and David, I travel from Köln through the night in a couchette with our ultimate destination, Nordhausen, but as the train is due there very early, we stay on board for two hours alighting at Lutherstadt Eisleben intending to travel back at a later hour. It is my first experi-

ence of an East German town and a major culture shock. It's an understatement to say *it has seen better times* as, formerly a centre of steel and coal, it is now devoid of heavy industry. We don't expect the place to be alive this early but are hungry and look for somewhere to eat; I would love to see a *Trabant* car and it takes time for both. We come across a bakery in a side street, a queue of people outside with baskets, which they fill with bread. On getting to the

My first view of East Germany: Lutherstadt Eisleben (author)

counter we see iced buns, and those in the queue look amazed as to how we can afford them. It's a quick

lesson into how bad things are for people in the East. Armed with our breakfast, we turn the corner and see four *Trabants* in a row. Reviled throughout the DDR, they are about to become a cult car. Back at the station, a coffee bar is open so we buy some to drink with our buns. This is how I start my first day in the former German Democratic Republic!

We take a westbound train, arrive at Nordhausen at eight o'clock, walk to the Harz station and the second departure of the day is waiting for us.

Left: a surprise early morning group of people dressed in medieval costume in animated discussion as they admire the Harzquerbahn tank locomotive on our train to Wernigerode (author)

Our train, hauled by a large tank locomotive, runs through to Wernigerode and leaves Nordhausen climbing steeply through a deep wooded valley before arriving at the first of two junctions, Eisfelder Talmühle, where a connection for Gernrode awaits.

The line continues through deeply forested country though it's not seen to best advantage due to the wet and overcast conditions. The next junction of Drei Annen Hohne is where the famous Brocken line comes in from the left. This goes to the highest point in the Harz Mountains where the Soviets had a radar listening station whose employees had to get there by train (I don't go there this time but am to return a year later for that journey). It is a short and steep downhill section from here to the terminus Wernigerode, which is also headquarters and main depot for the Harz system.

A scene full of atmosphere at Eisfelder Talmühle as connection is made to the Gernrode train (author)

Wernigerode is the centre of operations for the Harz system and has a sizeable locomotive depot and workshop. There are connections to a standard gauge line that originates at the border with West Germany at Stapelburg and runs to Halberstadt where it connects with the main line to Berlin. The town is attractive with a lot of half-timbered buildings. We have lunch and look around the depot before taking an afternoon train to Drei Annen Hohne and on to Eisfelder Talmühle.

Here we head east on the Gernrode line, diverging at Stiege on a branch to Hasselfelde, reverse back to Stiege then on to Gernrode, junction for a standard gauge line from Thale. That train is hauled by one of the ubiquitous former DDR diesel locomotives for the run to Quedlinburg, where we stay the night.

A quiet corner of the UNESCO World Heritage Town of Quedlinburg (author)

Culture and language clash that evening as I order a halibut steak at dinner; it arrives underdone twice over and I send it back; on the third occasion I hear an almighty crashing sound as my plate is being hurled across the kitchen. They get it right in the end, by which time my companions have finished their steaks!

That apart, Quedlinburg, an extraordinary town, its centre almost completely half-timbered, is about to be awarded UNESCO World Heritage status. I cannot think of a more appropriate place for this designation.

The following morning, we take a local train from Quedlinburg to Halberstadt (which David points out, literally translated means 'half a town') though it is a substantial place with its own tram system. From here, it is an express train to Berlin and a journey beyond that is to take us to Dresden, Prague and Vienna.

A year later, I return on a brief visit to the Harz system with Peter and I make a point of travelling to the Brocken, a mountain route ending at the site of a former Soviet Listening Station; with its steep climb it is the cream of the Harz system and its most used line. We stay a night in Wernigerode in a smart hotel whose prices are at least twice as high as Quedlinburg the previous year, but it now has ensuite accommodation. The train journey there is a revelation. From Hannover, we get a train to Bad Harzburg then a bus to Stapelburg in former East Germany where the train station is in the middle of a field! The direct link between Hannover and Wernigerode has since been restored throughout. The countryside and towns east of Stapelburg appear to be from another age and I reckon not much has changed since the 1930's; fascinating but not likely to stay like this for long.

Left: a feature of this weekend rail tour is the spectacular run-pasts, whereby passengers de-train, the train reverses and then storms toward the photographers. Probably the best of this trip is the first run-past over this fine viaduct near Thusis on the Chur-St Moritz main line (author)

My first introduction to the amazing Rhaetian Railway (RhB) system in south-east Switzerland is on a steam train in 1970. The whole system south of Chur has been electrified for fifty years and the restored steam locomotives have not been in active service most of that time. I will take the reader on two visits, travelling with my father in consecutive years 1970/1971 which between them cover about 80% of the route mileage. The centre of the Rhaetian system is the city of Chur where the SBB main line meets the metre-gauge Rhaetian line and branch to Arosa (the latter leaves from outside the station). Add trams and post buses and the station environs are a hive of activity.

Now add the steam train and the excitement is palpable on this September 1970 morning as we gather with others awaiting the arrival of our special excursion. It is a two-day itinerary; the first sees an amazing ride over the principal main line from Chur to Samedan. There are three steam locomotives provided; 2-8-0's 107 & 108 as train engines and 0-6-0 11 'Heidi' for banking and shunting assistance.

It is outside the peak season so that train pathing becomes easier. Even so, we have to await the departure of the famous *Glacier Express* at 09.15 hrs before we are given the OK. All three locomotives are with us for the initial 70 kms to Filisur as there are heavy grades and *Heidi* is at the rear to give assistance. The first 16 kms is jointly run with Furka Oberalp Bahn trains as far as Reichenau-Tamims, where the line heads into the mountains with spectacular structures. From here we are in Alpine country and the scenery is truly stunning. At Thusis we cross a northbound freight hauled by an electric locomotive. After leaving here, we are given opportunity to photograph a run-past on a spectacular viaduct. This is well organised; we all get off and position ourselves on a hillside with a view over the valley.

From Thusis to Filisur the line is still climbing through increasingly impressive mountain scenery. The best is to come after Filisur as we cross the Landwasser Viaduct, the railways' most famous icon where the line comes off the viaduct into a tunnel on a sheer rock face. Following this are spectacular spiral tunnels necessary to gain height rapidly. Later we spot three sharp mountain peaks ahead presaging the arrival at the Albula Tunnel, largest engineering feature of the line at 5,865 metres long. We stop at the south end of the tunnel for photographs to be taken of the train and for a scheduled service train to pass. This is again well organised with enough time for us to get above the tunnel to get better pictures. The Rhaetian Railway was first partly opened in the late 1880's operated by steam traction for the first 20 or so years followed by electric in 1904 thus our steam locomotives are over 80 years old.

Vintage *crocodile* electric locomotive at Samedan (author)

After Albula, the line drops sharply to the junction of Samedan where three lines diverge; to St Moritz, Tirano (Bernina line) and Scuols, the latter to be our final destination. Our train reverses, two locomotives leave and it continues on the more gently graded line to Scuols with just 108. This line is one of the last to be operated with RhB's *crocodile* electric locomotives and we pass one en route. We make another photo run-past stop at Zernez on a convenient curve with excellent visibility. The train will retrace this route next morning as far as Zernez, then take a roundabout route back to Chur via Klosters and Davos.

Scuols is where we stay the night and are allocated accommodation with locals: our host is Frau Roth, a cheery woman who offers good food and hospitality. There is no doubt that Scuols is a perfect Alpine town situated in a dramatic landscape of snow-covered mountains on three sides. We find it is quiet at this time of the year but evidently is busy during the winter ski season. There is talk of providing a direct rail route with a very long tunnel from Davos, which, if it comes to fruition, will surely spoil the tranquil beauty of the town and its valley so we enjoy it while we can. The next day's itinerary is to to return to Samedan and then to St. Moritz, most famous of all towns in Engadine and destination of choice for top stars of screen and stage; it looks fabulously prosperous though we get lunch here at a moderate price!

Right: Alpine beauty: the small town of Scuols is also a major ski resort but is quiet prior to the season (author)

The next day's itinerary is to retrace our route to Samedan and on to St. Moritz; from there it is back with 107 and 108 again as the route to Davos is heavily graded and proves to be spectacular though with fewer viaducts and tunnels than the Albula line. Davos and neighbouring Klosters are world-class skiing resorts, visited by the rich and famous. We leave them for the route back to Chur via Klosters and Landquart and as this is primarily downgrade, are back to one locomotive, 107. It has been an incredible trip over two days which we will remember for a long time.

Almost a year later, we are again in Scuols having arrived from Landquart in Austria on a hair-raising journey by *Europabus* twisting and turning on a road through the mountain passes. Next day we leave on an express to St. Moritz and after lunch take a train to Pontresina and the start of the famous Bernina line, one of the rack sections of the Rhaetian Railway (for good reason as we are soon to find). This is to be an amazing journey of stunning scenery along valley of the River Inn and the Lago Bianco which is a beautiful ultramarine blue. A tributary of the mighty Danube, the Inn used to create the blue of the river of the Strauss era.

The Lago Bianco and Bernina Pass as seen from the train (author)

It gets even more spectacular when we arrive at Alp Grüm and suddenly see the valley way down below us with a sheer cliff in between. This is where the rack system comes in as the line edges its way sideways down this cliff with a series of switchbacks and these continue for the next 8 kms. When we think it's all over there's more to come between as the line does a complete spiral in a final effort to reach the valley floor. We soon cross the Italian border to our terminus in Tirano and the end to another spectacular Alpine journey on the amazing Rhaetian Railway!

A brief postscript: unknown to us, Italian time is an hour different to Swiss so when we think it's a seventy-minute wait for our connection to Lecco; it is in fact ten minutes! In the meantime, we stroll into town and arrive back to find our train left an hour before. A hot, sweaty journey ensues in an ancient FS diesel railcar before reaching Lecco, one of the last outposts of Italian steam trains.

It is as part of a Railway Study Tour of southern Sweden organised by Paul Salveson in 2004 that I am introduced to a narrow gauge line to Vastervik on the Baltic Sea. Our base is the attractive town of Jönjöping on Lake Vättern in southern Sweden. The group has been studying the Swedish experiment in devolving and co-ordinating local passenger transport; it combines studies on the third day with an outing to a restored deeply rural line.

Jönjöping station by Lake Vattern; a *Green Cargo* train conveys *Ikea* products (author)

I am accompanied by Josiane and we start on a local train to Mariannelund via Nässjö, change to a bus for a short journey to Ankarsrum, principal intermediate station on a long, diesel operated, narrow-gauge* heritage route.   *It is just short of metre gauge at 891mm

We join our heritage railcar at Ankarsrum (author)

Travelling through countryside typified by dense coniferous forest, a landscape dotted with lakes, the 80 kms trip to Vastervik is fascinating, especially when we stop at Holt, a chalet-style station halfway along for lunch. The station, run by railway volunteer Karina Jonnson, has been converted into a honeymoon suite most tastefully and faithfully retains its historic features and we enjoy one of the most enchanting lunches imaginable. The line ends at the Baltic port of Vastervik and though Paul has arranged a visit to the depot, we opt to see the town which proves to be most attractive and historic and Josiane achieves a lifelong wish to see the Baltic Sea. There is a regular Swedish Railways train service here from Linköping.

Historic Vastervik on the Baltic Coast: A Y1 Fiat railcar is arriving from Linköping (author)

We return on our narrow-gauge railcar over the complete route of 120 kms to Hultsfred and the journey takes almost three hours; with scenery almost entirely forest it's fortunate that we are able to chat to friends to pass the time. Hultsfred is a significant junction where routes from Linköping and Nässjö join to continue to Kalmar on the Baltic coast. We have a short wait in pleasant sunshine here before taking a through train to Jönjöping; a memorable day!

Jönjöping train at Hultsfred. Our railcar has retired to the sidings for the night (author)

No German train journeys are included though DB has a huge intercity network (author)

Great Railway Journeys are to be had all over the European continent, though nowadays they are a lot less exciting: much faster, running over high-speed networks, lookalike trains, nothing *unique*. It was not always so as there are for many years the Trans European Express (TEE) trains and a fair number of international express trains; the *Orient Express*, the *Rheingold*, the *Puerta de Sol* to name a few.

Mostly, these trains charge supplements to travel and are sometimes first class only; this restricts me, always travelling on a budget though for second class, free (as a railway employee). I get to travel on two TEE's by paying a hefty supplement and these, the *Cisalpin* and *Catalan Talgo* are described in this chapter.

In North America as you will read in later chapters, where normal scheduled service is used, there are great train trips to be made, over long distances and several days, creating unique travel experiences.

I have taken a cross section of interesting long-distance trips in Europe as below, so join me for the ride!

- *Flèche d'Or* (Golden Arrow), Calais to Paris

- *Le Cisalpin*, Paris to Lausanne

- *Catalan Talgo*, Barcelona to Grenoble

- *Polar Express*, Trondheim to Bodø

- *Frecciarossa/Italo*, Milan to Florence

The *Flèche d'Or* recreated in 2002 as a London-Paris tour, seen here at Abbeville (author)

The *Flèche d'Or* is one of the first two trains I see at Calais in 1958 as our school group arrives in France for their holiday on the *Côte d'Azur*. Unfortunately, we are on the other train leaving ten minutes later and making several intermediate stops en route to Paris. Our 1959 school trip to Paris uses the Folkestone to Boulogne route and the train from there to Paris is hauled by a *Pacific* type locomotive but the rolling stock is truly awful (ex-Nord carriages with a slam door to every bay and metallic interior walls). The wag reporting the trip in the school magazine isn't far out when he writes '*we made Paris by cattle train*!'

The *Flèche d'Or* in steam days is a smart train complete with *Wagons-Lits* restaurant and first-class sleeping cars; second-class coaches and couchettes (the sleepers and couchettes being hauled around the Paris *Grande Ceinture* line from Gare du Nord to Gare de Lyon for attaching to a train to the *Côte d'Azur*). Both classes are subject to a supplementary charge. It operates to Paris with just one stop at Amiens which from 1959 onwards is for a locomotive change (electrification having taken place between Amiens and Paris).

Left: the scene at Calais Maritime in 1964. On the left is the *Flèche d'Or* hauled by an E-class Pacific, formerly of the Chemin de Fer du Nord. This leaves at 14.40 hrs and, with an Amiens stop, is due at Paris at 17.50 hrs. On the right is the slightly slower *Rapide* at 14.44 hrs arriving Paris at 18.08 hrs with three stops. It is hauled by a K-class Pacific, formerly of the PLM (Paris à Lyon et à la Méditerranée) (author)

The *Flèche d'Or* as a unique train runs until 1972, by which time it has succumbed to diesel locomotive haulage between Calais and Amiens (by pairs of BB 67000 class locomotives). However, its successor is a standard *Rapide* with a first-class Pullman coach, and for some years still includes a *Wagons-Lits* restaurant car as a remnant of its past glory. Though I see the train on a number of occasions, I never get to travel on the 'real thing' and my first journey on the successor *Rapide* is a trip to Paris for the Wales-France Rugby International in 1973 with Robert. It still has the luxury of a restaurant car where we enjoy a fine meal of 'rare' steak and frites and it is diesel-hauled as far as Amiens and electric beyond.

Left: the *Flèche d'Or* is electric-hauled between Amiens and Paris from 1959 up to its demise in 1972 by one of these handsome BB16000 locomotives. This is arriving at Amiens on the northbound train in September 1964; note the headboard is a simple affair with just the arrow and shield but no mention of the train's name. This scene is to continue from 1972 to 1994 when the *Rapide* service finally ceases with the inauguration of *Eurostar* (author)

Right: on the same day and minutes before the arrival of the train from Paris, two locomotives come from Longeau depot to take the *Flèche d'Or* to Calais (author)

From 14 November 1994, *Eurostar* service via the Channel Tunnel commences and the *Rapide* between Calais and Paris runs its final trip. The new order is much faster and journey time between London and Paris is halved at a stroke; it's the end of an era.

On 12 October 2002, a special is arranged to celebrate 75 years since inauguration of this famous train and I travel on the outward journey. It is a great trip, steam hauled by ex-Southern *Battle of Britain* class locomotive to Dover, the *m.v. Canterbury*, Dover Eastern Docks to Calais Maritime and a 231K *Pacific* Calais Ville to Paris. The only non-authentic part is the bus transfer at Dover and Calais, the dock stations having closed. The train loses time progressively in France, bizarrely due to the locomotive firebox having a negative effect on hot axle box detectors.

The *Flèche d'Or* leaving Gare du Nord on 13 Oct 2002 (author)

The *Cisalpin* is one of the famous *Trans Europe Express (TEE)* trains that crisscrossed the continent for many years. All are first class with supplements payable on top so they are not cheap. They are to succumb by the late '90's first to a wider network of *Eurocity* trains and later (and finally) by the growth of Europe's high speed rail network and the likes of TGV's.

In 1970, I make my first of two trips on TEE trains accompanied by my father and throw caution to the winds as we take the *Cisalpin* between Paris and Lausanne in Switzerland. The train continues to Milan through the Swiss Alps. Our own journey is to continue through Switzerland to the Rhaetian Railway for

its steam train specials (chap. 9). The train is formed of a dual-voltage electric multiple-unit train built specially for TEE operations (and is to be replaced by locomotive-hauled trains four years later). Leaving Paris Gare de Lyon at 12.20 hrs, it goes down the PLM main line to its first stop at Dijon two hours later, during which we enjoy an excellent lunch in the dining car. After Dijon, it is a very scenic journey through the mountainous Jura region. Apart from this, there are only two other daytime express trains on this line through the sparsely populated region. Our next stop is Val-

lorbe, a border town with Switzerland, arriving four hours after leaving Paris. From there, the train drops down with fine views of Lake Geneva and forty minutes later, arrives at Lausanne, a very busy city where we alight. It's been an interesting experience.

Left: the *Catalan Talgo* (on left) in 1975 is overpowered by the size of Barcelona Termino's train shed, its *Talgo* coaches out of sight. Once the main terminus in the city, that has shifted to *Sants* station (author)

Below right: the famous *Sagrada Familia* cathedral makes for a bizarre sight in Barcelona (author)

Below left: surrounded on most sides by the French Alps, Grenoble presents a complete contrast to Barcelona (author)

Five years after my first TEE trip, an opportunity to travel on another train in the group comes when my father and I need to get from Barcelona to Grenoble for a steam rail tour next day. Being a complex routing, there is a convenient through train, the *Catalan Talgo*, which leaves Barcelona around 10.00 hrs for an eight-hour journey. It travels through Girona to the French border at Port Bou/Cerbère then along the Mediterranean coast through Narbonne to Avignon, up the Rhône Valley to Valence, then cross-country to Grenoble, an interesting and varied itinerary. As the Cerbère-Narbonne and Valence-Grenoble sections are not electrified, a diesel locomotive runs through from Cerbère to Grenoble;

with an electric from Barcelona to Port Bou. The train is formed of *Talgo* coaches of a unique articulated design and suspension, low slung and capable of gauge changing. It is a fascinating and comfortable journey, and we have lunch in the dining car along the Mediterranean coast. Arrival at Grenoble is in an entirely different landscape of snow-laden Alps and it is much cooler.

Left: *Nohab* diesel locomotive waiting to depart Trondheim on the 08.00 hrs to Bodø; the journey is to take almost 12 hours (author)

I visit Scandinavia for the first time in 1972 accompanied by Chris. Norway's reputation for spectacular mountain and coastal scenery and equally spectacular railway journeys goes before it. Arriving at Bergen, the route to Oslo and its branch line to Flåm is our first introduction to the wonders of its railways, then from Oslo to Trondheim. In my view the best is still to come; the 730 kms far north route to Bodø. Unusually for Norway, it is not electrified, and its northern part is relatively new, Bodø not being reached until 1954; the original intention was a strategic route to Narvik but the money ran out.

The first landmark is Hell, where we leave the Stockholm line and strike north; the scenery changes from hilly countryside interspersed with coastal sections and there is still a lot of snow around. Surprisingly, I notice substantial industry in several places for the production of steel and aluminium. We cross the Arctic Circle about halfway up, the sign announcing it knee deep in snow. A feature of the train is its restaurant car serving the best halibut steak I've had anywhere. Near journeys' end is Fauske where the line turns left: it should have gone straight on north to Narvik but the terrain is unforgiving, hence the decision in 1954 to strike west to Bodø. On arrival at this attractive port town, we stay the night and plan to sail to the Lofotens and then overnight on a small ferry to Narvik next day.

Left: arrival at Bodø is just before 20.00 hrs and due to its far north position, it is still bright daylight (author)

Right: from here, we travel to the Lofoten Islands on the *Erling Jarl* seen at the end of Bodø's main street (author)

Left: high-speed trains in competition! On the left is NTV's *Italo* and in the centre FS's *Frecciarossa* (Red Arrow); at far right is an FS local train. The location is attractively-named *Santa Maria Novella* station in Florence (Firenze) named after the Basilica near the station

The final journeys in this chapter are also some of my most recent in Europe. In 2016, Josiane and I take a holiday in Bologna and we fly to Milan, take the bus to Milano Centrale station and travel on a pre-booked *Frecciarossa* for the one-hour, 215 kms run to Bologna. I am excited but temper with my previous experiences with Italian Railways which have generally not been very good. I am to be pleasantly surprised both by the sleek, beautifully designed, train and the on-board service which is excellent. Timekeeping is perfect, so I reckon FS has turned the corner. Is it, I wonder, due to competition from private company NTV marketed as *Italo* and paralleling most of FS's high speed operations?

I decide to find out. At Bologna, NTV has a roving ticket sales lady who books me with my credit card on the spot but not before a lot of questions about discounts (regrettably, offered only a day or more in advance). So I pay up and we travel second class on the 92 kms, 35 minute journey to Firenze, 90% in tunnel through the scenic Apennines! My verdict is, it's not as good as FS with poor on-board service. Also, on return we are diverted to the old line taking over an hour due to an incident on the HS route (which they did not explain or apologise for). It is dark so we still don't see the Apennines!

Right: Bologna Centrale is the major railway crossroads in northern Italy. Most high speed trains now use a new underground station but some still use the old station. Here, a *Frecciabianca* (high speed conventional train) from Ancona to Milano arrives. Another high speed service is the *Frecciaargento* which runs on both high-speed and conventional lines (author)

11　Coastal Cruising

without the glamour and high prices

Notwithstanding my great love of travel, I have never been attracted to cruising, the idea of a floating hotel with everything done for you and the sheer luxury of it just doesn't appeal. However, twice in my travelling life, opportunities have presented themselves for travelling on public service coastal steamers, in both cases along the west coasts in the north of two continents; and I have taken them and persuaded a like-minded companion to accompany me each time.

First the *Hurtigrute*, a daily steamer service up the coast of Norway from Bergen to the Russian frontier which is the lifeline for numerous isolated coastal and island communities and defers to the tourist with a first-class section with extras for those who come to see outstanding landscapes. Second and some eighteen years later the *Alaska Marine Highway*, which, whilst acting as a lifeline to a number of island communities, is more of a long-distance car ferry for visitors to the south western part of Alaska. The two are different in the markets they aim to serve but both have a common outcome of cruising on a budget (the price is less but it's the same great scenery!).

There is another element which appeals to me as it is more of a DIY experience and holds a challenge.

The genesis of this 1973 trip is twofold; firstly from my first ever visit to Scandinavia in 1972, part of which was a short hop across the channel to the Lofoten Islands on the coastal steamer; secondly, a desire, shared by Brian for a photographic trip on the Norwegian coast at the time of the midnight sun.

The outcome is a journey of a lifetime, evidently so as I am writing about it forty-seven years later, almost as clear in my mind like it was yesterday. It's an adventure as we share the voyage with all manner of people and witness a human and trade lifeline to Norway's remote outposts with an incredible scenic backdrop. We achieve a key objective of seeing the midnight sun and have a follow up one-way ticket to Hell!

The *m.v. Polarlys* is one of a fleet of thirteen steamers on the *Hurtigrute* (author)

It all starts on a wet evening on the last day of June as Brian and I set sail from Bergen, Norway's principal port. Our ship for the next ten days is *m.v. Erling Jarl*, co-incidentally the same that Chris and I sailed on from Bodø to Svolvær last year. It is one of the older vessels in a fleet of thirteen, well built with good facilities. We are allocated cabins with a seaward viewthough the portholes are too small to make it a useful sightseeing option. The cabin has washing facilities though toilets and bathroom (with old fashioned bath) are down the corridor. As tourists we are automatically first class with better facilities than regulars. The dining lounge is a step up from the cafeteria with its buffet style *smörgåsbord* for all meals; there is a tourist lounge where we can and do mix with other travellers from all over the world.

We wake next morning to the sight of an offshore island and a stylish road bridge linking it to the mainland. The breakfast table is a sight for sore eyes, smoked fish and cold cuts, fruit, open sandwiches; an inviting *smörgåsbord*. We are already getting a good feeling about this journey which takes a routing between mainland and islands, stopping periodically at remote settlements, some with time to make shore excursions. Later, we call at the coastal town of Ålesund and an excursion to the town.

As midnight approaches, though the weather is overcast, it is evident that we are close to the midnight sun as we are in our cabins before darkness sets in.

We wake on the third day to find the ship already docked at Trondheim where it is due to spend six hours, the time needed to load and unload freight; a realisation that the main purpose of the ships is serving remote communities for residents and their everyday needs. We take a shore excursion to see the city and its fine cathedral. On return, we see southbound ferry *m.v. Kong Olav* already docked further up the quay.

Departing at mid-day, we go to the restaurant where a sumptuous *smörgasbord* is on offer, more ambitious with a cold table and some hot dishes, various fish and meat offerings with salads and dressings. I decide to try the whale meat which it must be admitted doesn't look tempting and tastes even less so, old boots spring to mind: *whale meat again*? (apologies to Vera Lynn); I don't think so! The afternoon journey takes us past some incredibly beautiful islands like Stoksund which look stunning in the afternoon sunshine.

Early next morning is Nesna, a mainland settlement and it is here that, shortly after docking, a large rather scraggy dog trots down to the quay looking expectantly upwards whereupon the kitchen crew toss out a bag of waste food which the dog grabs with alacrity and trots contentedly up the main street. Six days later on our southbound journey, we call at mid-day and sure enough, down trots the dog again; the mystery is, with two ferries and two square meals a day, how come the dog is so scraggy?

Right: there is some excitement as we pass the symbol denoting the Arctic Circle (known here as the Polarsirkelen. The previous year I had seen a similar symbol on the far north railway line (author)

Later that day we cross the Arctic Circle marked by a half globe and arrow symbol on a promontory to our left. We also join in to experience the tradition of having iced water poured over our heads paying respect to Neptune. It is again a spectacular coast and we see more fjords penetrating into the mainland. At mid-day, we arrive at Bodø, where I join the same ship a year ago for the journey to Svolvaer.

The weather up to now has been variable with both rain and sunshine and is about to get worse as we leave Bodø. This is the only part of the voyage with a long crossing of open sea toward the Lofotens. Before supper I decide to take a bath and at the same time the ship starts tossing violently in the storm; through the porthole I can see the turbulent sea and as I reach for my towel, feel cold water on the floor and panic.

It's as well as it will be embarrassing for me to dash into the corridor clad in just a towel. I get dressed and join Brian for dinner. At this point, it's worth mentioning what a fine *smörgåsbord* is provided at dinner, hot meat and fish dishes supplementing the cold table; this evening it is doubly welcome to compensate for the inclement weather. After dinner, the storm has abated, and we go on deck to see sister ship *Harald Jarl* on a southbound trip having just left Stamsund.

Left: out of the gloom appears the *m.v. Harald Jarl* in stormy waters on a southbound *Hurtigrute* service Behind are the menacing mountains of the Lofoten Islands (author)

The Lofoten Islands loom menacingly, and we are soon in Stamsund. Between there and the principal town of Svolvær, we pass the eerie cliffs of Raftsund, entrance to the *Trollfjord* of Nordic myth and legend; it is 22.00 hrs and still daylight. Waiting for skies to clear, we and many others are on deck either side of midnight looking for a miracle; it doesn't happen! The ship makes a number of calls during the day at small towns and villages as it has left the open sea and is back between mainland and islands with Tromsø the next significant port of call. This gateway to the Arctic is starting point of many great polar adventurers. A stop of nearly four hours here gives time for a shore excursion.

Right: Tromsø's stunning Arctic Cathedral dominates the skyline; its design gives new meaning to *avant-garde!* (author)

We tour the city incorporating a panoramic view from above and the highlight is the Arctic Cathedral. Many other buildings are

modern in style and the whole effect leaves me impressed that this place knows how to live it up. Another evening of expectations and dashed hopes as the sun again fails to appear at midnight and we miss the most northerly city in the world as the Hammerfest call is in the small hours.

We look forward to Honnigsvåg, where an excursion takes us to the North Cape and a native Sami village. First, the short distance to the North Cape, the impressive northernmost point of the European mainland where it's quite cold. On the way back to Honnigsvåg, we call in on an encampment where a group of Sami live; they dress very colourfully and give us a friendly wave though they must see a lot of visitors given the ships run every day.

This far north, there are fewer islands and our journey is coast-hopping in and out of remote towns and villages, the last of which before nightfall (sic) is Berlevåg which turns out to be most interesting. Its port is in shallow waters so a 'tender' has to come out to the ship to ferry passengers and freight to and from the village. It's a really lovely sight in the calm waters of the bay and the sun is shining.

Its arrival gets us anticipating a 'midnight sun' at last and at the third attempt, it happens (*right*); sadly, Brian and I seem to be the only ones to witness it. Makes it all worthwhile and we sleep soundly, happy to have achieved our principal aim. The ship is now heading south east towards the Russian frontier having rounded the most northerly point. We arrive at Kirkenes at 06.00 hrs and a bus is waiting to take us to the frontier and back in time for a 09.30 hrs departure. They needn't have bothered as through the tall electric fence there is nothing to see other than *steppe*; not even worth a photograph but I can say I've been to Russia (almost). The schedule by accident or design takes us to places in daytime where it is night on the

outward journey. The journey to Berlevåg is unremarkable in that there are few mountains and fjords on the north coast. When we reach there, the northbound ship m.v. *Polarlys* is about to leave and the tender

comes to service our ship as before.

By midday, we are at Hammerfest, the northernmost town in the World with some time to explore. My recollection is not its fine church but the stuffed (well I think it is stuffed!) polar bear being stroked by a fearless kid.

We arrive at Tromsø before midnight and it's cloudy again so we don't see the sun but the city is as light as day (do they have 'nightlife' here in summer, one wonders?) and we are asleep by the time the ship leaves port. At breakfast next day, we reach Harstad, an attractive mountain backed location and third largest town in northern Norway. We sail down the eastern side of the islands in bright sunshine and it is remarkably warm when we arrive at the attractive town of Stokmarknes where see a young lad on the quay dressed only in a pair of shorts. The ship's crew issues us with fishing rods and suggests we fish for our supper. I have never been a successful angler and this evening is no exception; in a sea full of fish, I catch none, though fortunately Brian catches two and we have them cooked for dinner later.

The amazing Trollfjord, stuff of Norse legend *(shutterstock)*

We call at Svolvær in early evening whilst eating our dinner of freshly caught fish and on leaving here, enjoy stunning views of the Lofoten mountains over again and it's nice to see the *Trollfjord* in sunlight. This time, the ship sails up the fjord, the sheer walls of which are so narrow that the ship makes a 180 degree turn by underwater propulsion jets. Stamsund is reached just before midnight and the sun is still shining! We cross the Vestfjorden between Stamsund and Bodø in calmer waters than on the outward trip and get an undisturbed sleep, seeing nothing of Bodø.

Torghatten, the rock with a hole (author)

Later, we pass a landmark to our right missed on the outward journey; a rock known as Torghatten which has a hole through the middle, reputed to have been made by a giant viking arrow piercing through. A more rational reason for this geological feature exists but we are not told this. This is our last night at sea and our voyage comes to an end on arrival at Trondheim in the morning. We have been on *Erling Jarl* for just over ten days and the journey of our dreams.

We have managed to avoid hell on sea, but we are about to witness the real place on earth. The following morning, we explore Trondheim's attractive maritime quarter and after lunch, go to the station to get the train to Hell (this is a first for me as I've often travelled on the train *from Hell*). It is a single diesel railcar, and we ask the guard for two round trip tickets; silly us, you can only get one-way tickets to Hell!

Left: so this is HELL with just me and Brian to prove that it's not so bad, is it? It is raining, but at least not coals of fire on our heads (well, if that's what Hell is really like, count me in for the afterlife!). The views from here are stunning, which for all the world could be a railway junction on the Cambrian Coast line. We take the same train back an hour later and the guard has no problem issuing one-way tickets back to Trondheim. Some years later, the old goods forwarding sign is re-erected. In Norwegian, it reads 'HELL GODS - EXPEDITION! (author)

The *Erling Jarl* at Molde on our journey north (author)

Having visited Alaska for the first time in 1988 with great caution (after all, it's a long way back if you don't like it), Peter and I opt for just three days in the state. A big mistake as we are both smitten and vow to return for a longer period sometime in the future.

The *Matanuska* at Bellingham, Washington is to be our home for the next three days (author)

That time arrives in 1991, when, following a period in California, we travel north to Seattle on Amtrak's *Coast Starlight* and are to join the ship leaving from Bellingham, two hours north of Seattle, the next day. I recall sitting in our hotel that evening as it rains heavily outside and the weather forecast on TV gives a picture of unremitting gloom as a trough of low pressure is set for a few days more.

So, to our great relief, the day dawns bright, sunny and set fair for a good journey. We are heading to Bellingham, two hours journey north of Seattle on a *Greyhound* bus. As we find so often in America, conversation with fellow passengers is normal and we chat to a man from Texas who is taking his son travelling around America. He tells me I'm Welsh, to which I of course agree, but how does he know? *'Do you know Treharris'*, he asks. I say I do though it's only a small valleys town off the beaten track. *'I was there a few weeks ago visiting my cousin, Mr Parry, who owns the local pharmacy. Be sure to look him up when you get back and say Hi'*. His name is Renée, one I can't forget as it is the central character in the TV comedy *Allo, Allo*! We say farewell to Renée and son at Bellingham as we alight and walk to the quayside to see our ship the *m.v.Matanuska* waiting. On board we go to our cabin at the rear; Peter has only been able to reserve this two-weeks earlier and the alternative would have meant sleeping on deck! We had wondered what this might be like until we see deck passengers with frame tents (no pegs, weighed down by rucksacks!). It is quite a large ferry with room for cars and catering is a very lively cafeteria style which is cheap and cheerful.

Steerage class on the *Matanuska* (author)

Our voyage starts in early afternoon and is to take three and a half days to Juneau, State Capital of Alaska, calling on the way at four island ports off the coast of Alaska. For the rest of the day we sail in Canadian waters off the west coast of Vancouver Island and by nightfall still in Canadian territory. The atmosphere on board is relaxing as the fine warm weather has held and it's just like a cruise. We talk to many people, including a Methodist minister from Virginia, who it turns out has a friend in Swansea whom he has visited; she lives in St James' Crescent, a place I pass daily on my way to work. We also meet a young man from Cardiff making a return trip for a kayaking holiday in Alaska.

When we wake next day, are back in USA territory having passed Prince Rupert in the early hours and shortly to arrive at Ketchikan, our first morning call. Hemmed in by mountains, the town is accessed only by air and sea and has a long history, originally settled by native Tlingit. We head back out to sea with the islands to the east of us; it is a day and night journey to our next call, Sitka, through the most amazing land and seascapes. Things are getting lively on board as passengers are encouraged to do forty circuits of the ship to walk a mile and there are many contenders for the record. The atmosphere is very friendly and in true American fashion, we talk to many more people.

Sunset over the Gulf of Alaska (author)

After another night at sea, we make land at our second call, Sitka, a native Tlingit village developed back in the days of Russian ownership of Alaska. It is in an idyllic setting and we get a couple of hours ashore to explore and learn about its fascinating history, photograph the Russian Orthodox Church and other landmarks.

A group of children, of American and Tlingit origin, get their photo taken and are lucky to live in this paradise (author)

It is unbelievably beautiful as we weave our way between the islands and mainland as we head back east to reach our next port of call, Wrangell, in late afternoon. We are allowed a couple of hours ashore and take a walk for some distance to see a large colony of nesting sea eagles. It is a surprise to see the young birds are brown in colour and appear to be bigger than the parents which are white with a bald patch on their heads. Even in remote areas like this, I have to be on my guard. A pick-up truck stops, and the driver menacingly accuses me of taking his photograph earlier; I keep my cool, say I've never seen him before, and he moves on. From Wrangell, we head north-west in the evening, closer to the mainland and weave our way through the archipelago and it is night-time when we make our final intermediate call at Petersburg.

The *Matanuska* at berth in Wrangell, Alaska (author)

As we wake on the third morning, it is steaming past Admiralty Island, a heavily forested National Monument and head north-east up the strait leading later to the narrow passageway to Skagway, the eventual destination of our ship.

Light aircraft are a very common sight over Alaska (author)

At the approach to Auke Bay, the port for Juneau, the captain advises us to look for whales, common hereabouts, but unfortunately, we don't catch sight of any. We land in Auke Bay and are met by a bus that will take us the ten miles into Juneau while the ship continues on to Skagway, and what a journey this turns out to be! Our driver, looking like one of the pioneers with baseball cap and rough beard is obviously a redblooded capitalist who, throughout the journey, keeps up a narrative suggesting that all people in Juneau except him are government employees or dependents who don't know the meaning of hard work and out to justify their own existence, entertaining stuff! Juneau, though not the largest city in Alaska is nonetheless the State Capital. We leave Juneau by air two days later to explore deeper into the wonderful interior of Alaska, the Denali National Park and view the USA's highest mountain, 20,250 foot Mount Denali but that's another story.

Evening sets in as we approach Auke Bay, the port for Juneau (author)

Inevitably ones' inaugural visit to a place or country is of greater interest and significance than subsequent ones as everything is new, exciting and very different to ordinary life. My first visit to North America is a high point in my travels and I immerse myself in new cultural and geographical experiences, keep a fairly detailed diary and timeline highlighting the high- and low-points.

There is little doubt I anticipated Canada would be more interesting than the USA and I couldn't have been more wrong! Canada is less of a culture shock and has a lot in common with the UK though is not as exciting as I expect. In contrast the USA is informal, wacky and welcoming with a strong willingness by people to please and a very commercial outlook on life; that is a big surprise. However, public services and their servants can be just as inefficient and awkward, sometimes more so, than in the UK.

Travel

The thrill of travelling vast distances overnight or several nights is a great adventure. Trains, some still bearing their original names, are instrumental in the opening up of this vast continent and connecting far distant places with each other. As a group they become the lifeblood of the continent; that under Amtrak they form a homogenous network doesn't detract from each route retaining its unique characteristics.

The eastbound *San Francisco Zephyr* at Ogden, Utah in June 1978 (author)

Big changes follow in the USA and Canada after the 1940's as air travel and interstate highways grow apace and edge trains from many long-distance routes. The situation becomes so serious in both countries that the state steps in. In the USA, the National Rail Passenger Corporation, Amtrak is set up in 1971 to ensure survival of a basic train network. Somewhat later in Canada, VIA Rail Canada is established to amalgamate former Canadian Pacific and Canadian National passenger services.

The State of Public Transport

As a transport professional, I cannot help noticing what it's like even when on holiday. North America in 1978 presents a sorry sight for public transport. There are few long-distance trains, often running less than daily; shorter distance intercity trains only one or at most a few per day; commuter networks generally peak hours only with a token - or no - service off-peak and weekends. The only bright spot is the North-East Corridor (Boston-New York-Washington) which generally has all day service of reasonable frequency.

Left: this photograph sums up the sorry state of train commuting in New York in 1982. Hoboken in New Jersey, connected by ferry across the Hudson River from Manhattan, is the terminus for travellers from wealthy suburbs who get a raw deal as no investment has been put in for years. Fortunately, a New Jersey Transit agency is set up and brings much needed investment in subsequent years (author)

Though main line passenger trains are improving with some hope for the future, most local transport is dire. I am shaken by what little is left of commuter networks on the east coast: Massachusetts, New York, New Jersey and Pennsylvania remain and a few cities have subways or trams. Elsewhere in the USA, just Illinois and California have commuter rail; *Metra* serving Chicago is in good shape with investment in rolling stock and a service ethic which puts the customer first. In Canada, Toronto has a commuter network in which the city region is investing heavily (*Go Transit*) and trams. Montreal has a modern metro, but its suburban rail network is no better than most USA systems and there's little sign of investment.

Right: in San Francisco, there is just one commuter line extant, the Southern Pacific *Peninsula Line* to San Jose, which hangs on long enough to be taken on by state-sponsored *CalTrain* and expanded service is evidenced by this photograph in San Francisco in 1991. It is still just the 46 kms Peninsula line but elsewhere in the state, *CalTrain* and other agencies bring massive growth in local transit (author)

The early 1980's is when metropolitan areas realise their economies are suffering from poor connectivity and recognise a need for public subsidy. Over the period of my visits to North America, I see major improvements to urban transit, city systems overhauled, and completely new networks created. My early experience of travel on city systems is limited to New York, Boston, Chicago and San Francisco. New York's subway is scary but also utterly fascinating and exciting; I even buy the t-shirt with the inscription *I rode the New York subway and survived*! A number of cities retain vintage trams, some simply as they haven't invested in replacements. New Orleans has made its heritage streetcars a major visitor attraction.

Left: some cities retain vintage trams, often because they haven't invested in replacements; New Orleans combines visitor attraction and mainstream transit with their heritage Streetcars (author)

Right: one route is immortalised in Tennessee Williams' play *A Streetcar named Desire* and I discover it must have been taken from a destination blind, now carried by a bus. *A Bus named Desire*? I don't think so! (author)

For medium and long distance travel, Amtrak's limited network is extant on the main trans-continental routes though is a fraction of the golden years of the 1950's when trains were top of their game. The introduction of *Superliner* double-deck rolling stock is a massive shot in the arm to long-distance travel, restoring some of its lost glamour. Trains in the east (with a more restrictive gauge) get *Amfleet* single level coaches, used on most trains in the north-east corridor (Boston-Washington) and some in the mid-west and west. Heritage rolling stock is still common though being phased out; some of it is showing its age and that can make journeys unpleasant, particularly if the air-conditioning is faulty or inoperable. The situation in

Right: VIA Rail's *Champlain*, an LRC train, on arrival at Quebec St Foy, a basic station almost six miles from the city centre. This happens as the old city centre stations' real estate value is judged to make it more important for commercial development as little future is seen for passenger trains. The same situation obtains in Canada's capital city, Ottawa; it's unbelievable! (author)

Canada is less developed with most trains still formed of heritage rolling stock. My journey on the *Canadian* is in un-refurbished coaches dating from the 1950's. The advent of VIA Rail in the late 1970's, several years later than Amtrak, partly explains the situation as investment in passenger trains is yet to begin in Canada. It first appears in 1980 with introduction of LRC (Light, Rapid, Comfortable) trains on the Montreal-Toronto axis and feeder routes. The situation on long-distance routes remains largely unchanged; the oldest rolling stock is withdrawn and the remainder refurbished as VIA Rail decides to promote tourist travel seriously.

Rolling stock, old and new in both countries, is good to travel in with lots of leg room and comfortable, uni-directional seats. Intercity and long-distance trains are mandated to have on board catering which is rigorously maintained. I recall joining the *Wolverine* at Detroit when the *Amcafé* steward asks me if I know the price of breakfast burgers. Really! The regular steward hasn't come in and it seems his replacement is hauled from the office to cover without formal training!

The provision and quality of catering is good, particularly restaurant cars though there is flip-flopping over the years between 'freshly cooked on board' or 'microwaved' in elusive attempts to make a profit. *Superliner* operated trains have lounge/bar cars with upstairs seats facing outward to aid sightseeing. Sleeping accommodation comes in two or three types depending on people's budgets though it isn't cheap. I and my companions often opt for reclining seats on overnight trips. On later trips with Josiane, reclining seats are not an option, so we book a first-class package: a roomette converting from a day to overnight use and inclusive of all meals. This is why long-distance travel is so agreeable despite problems with poor timekeeping and service disruption, an unfortunate feature on some trips.

1 Standard coach

2 Superliner sightseer lounge

3 Dining car

4 Roomette/sleeper

Accommodations on Amtrak trains are generally attractive as seen in the above photos from their website.

Travel on other modes

I don't travel on internal flights except to and within Alaska, where flying is often the *only* way. Other short distance flights are extensions to or from transatlantic routes.

Left: Alaska Airlines flight from Juneau to Anchorage at Yakutat. Air travel is an absolute lifeline for this State (author)

My experience on the Alaskan flights is mixed. *Northwest* has a reputation for overbooking and consequent *bouncing* offering passengers cash back to take a later flight; this is experienced and resisted on my first outbound flight from Seattle to Anchorage. By contrast, internal operator *Mark Air* gives superb service with no hassle. Three years later, state operator *Alaska Airlines* is also trouble free on a flight from Juneau to Anchorage. In the USA, whilst air travel is undoubtedly quicker and used by the majority, it doesn't enable seeing the fabulous landscapes, thus is of little interest to me.

Left: a *Greyhound* intercity bus at Seattle bus station. The buses carry a very distinctive livery and have become an icon in American travel, appearing prominently in films such as *Midnight Cowboy* with *Dustin Hoffman*. I find them comfortable and inviting (author)

Buses are used for some journeys where the train is not a viable option and I find service is generally good. The famous *Greyhound* is bus carrier of choice (often the only one) and I also experience *Trailways*. *Greyhound* is used between Vancouver and Seattle as Amtrak isn't yet on that route; otherwise, the bus is used from Cincinnati, Ohio to Lexington, Kentucky and Lamar to Denver, Colorado. Over the years, Amtrak develops its network of *Thruway* buses connecting with and between trains which I use occasionally, particularly in California. Local buses, plentiful though of dubious quality in cities, are sparse or non-existent in small towns. I find in Charleston, South Carolina, they appear to be used almost uniquely by black people.

Right: my first rental car, a Ford *Pinto* in Rocky Mountain National Park. It is the first time I drive an automatic and takes some getting used to! (author)

Rental cars are used mainly to tour the countryside and National Parks; American roads can be very variable. We rarely use *Interstates* as they are not generally of use in our itineraries and State highways are mostly good with an almost universal 55 mph speed limit and a variety of surveillance tactics to check on speeding, including from the air. Roads of lower categories are often poorly maintained and roughly surfaced, particularly in rural areas. In rural Kentucky, a state highway shown on the map peters out after 30 miles of abortive driving as it comes to a river! In Alaska, as I might have known, some highways are only safe for four-wheel drives. One feature common to all roads is the speed signposting and the way it changes to reflect traffic conditions. On a main road through town, speeds can vary up and down between 10 and 30 mph. Most urban roads are wide, a relic of the 19th century when the highway had to be wide enough to turn a horse and carriage without reversal!

People and Society

Welcome

Just how welcoming is America? When it comes to entering the country, it depends on whether it is the USA or Canada. The USA can be hostile, and nothing exemplifies this more than my initial arrival in New York. Expecting everything to be new and exciting, my introduction to what I imagine is the 'land of the free' is marred by huge immigration delays at Kennedy Airport. Everyone's name is checked against a book listing undesirables and enemies of the USA though Paul and I manage to pass through unscathed.

Maybe this is just New York which has a reputation for directness and plain speaking. Well, no, because subsequently, particularly coming from Canada, the long bureaucratic processes appear to be mutual, presumably the Canadians giving 'tit for tat'. When I arrive in Canada direct from the UK it is bureaucratic but not hostile. The encounters are the nature of governors rather than governed, for people in general, particularly in the USA, go out of their way to be helpful with a service ethic that leaves the British to shame.

America is violent? I initially believe this to be true and on my first night in New York, it takes time to venture out of the hotel until I realise, with thousands thronging the streets, the chance of getting mugged is slim; pickpocketing, yes, as Josiane finds to her cost when her handbag disappears near Times Square in New York.

Left: A great night out in a Times Square restaurant ends badly as Josiane's handbag goes missing *(shutterstock)*

In my nine visits to America, only once do I hear the sound of shooting and that is in Boston, a city I consider civilised! On my first visit, I am reluctant to leave Chicago Union station between changing trains due to its 'gangster' reputation (*Al Capone* was nearly forty years previous!). At our first hotel in New York, I learn to be vigilant in spotting and calling out petty crime. Sleep is interrupted by a telephone call from *Jeanie*; Paul, guessing this is a pro on the prowl, suggests *'Genie should get back in her bottle'* and that is the end of the call! For our first breakfast in New York, why not room service? Our order is telephoned, delivered and paid for; we are undersupplied and overcharged and by the time we realise our room waiter is long gone!

Twice in motels there are identical experiences that warn us to watch our step; in Detroit and Los Angeles, the receptionist is behind bars and it seems they need to be protected from unwelcome guests. In both places, it is some way through dimly lit streets to find our supper and in Los Angeles a translation is needed as the menu is in Japanese.

Travelling out of Los Angeles on a train, we are told of our foolishness in having gone to a Mexican market; at Ogden, in deepest Mormon country, we are warned not to walk the streets at night. In neither case do we see any signs of trouble so it's down to perception. On my final day in New York, I'm on my own in a Penn Station diner at a circular counter with bar stools. I don't finish lunch as I am being eyed by a suspicious man opposite who looks like he's heavy on drugs and my feeling is he's going to draw a gun at any moment and shoot me!

People

My impression of American people is good. Public and customer service employees, with whom we come into contact, are mainly conscientious and helpful. Transport people vary from helpful to apathetic; on a journey lasting several days, getting the right steward can make or break the experience.

Train ticket clerks in my experience, can be a pretty cynical bunch. On my first day in New York, I come across an expert in the craft when queuing for tickets at the office at Grand Central Station. The man in front is trying to buy tickets for himself and son, his credit card isn't verifying properly, and he's irritated. The clerks' response: *'okay smartarse, I'm doing my best, you'll just have to wait'* and I'm thinking, follow that, especially as I have to negotiate two one-way tickets to Montreal with 50% vouchers!

Even though each year we buy three-week travel passes, every journey must be ticketed 'free', an avoidable hassle but it's the system! It can have a humorous side as Josiane and I get ticketed for the *Coast Starlight* at Santa Barbara; the train is running late and the obliging young agent, seeing as we are English (he's wrong as Josiane is French and I am Welsh!), assumes we are into 'crop circles' as he evidently is, talks about his craze for this phenomenon and is *so* disappointed that we have only a passing enthusiasm.

In New Orleans a new experience is when we come across a political rally by the Democrats for the 2000 Presidential Election; we head to Jackson Square, where their nominee Al Gore is giving a speech on a balcony of a civic building. He is less than inspiring ,and the crowds call for *Tipper* who, it turns out, is Gore's wife. She gives a really rousing speech and gets supporters animated, sometimes frenzied; maybe she should be running for President!

Left: New Orleans Jackson Square & civic buildings *(shutterstock)*

Whilst in New Orleans, we need to visit a chiropractor; our hotel refers us to a Mr Michael whose practice is further up St Charles Avenue. Enquiring how to get there, his receptionist advises taking the streetcar and where to alight; it's amazing in an American city to be recommend public transport! Josiane warms to Mr Michael as he's the most interested and empathetic chiropractor in her experience. Years later, when Hurricane Katrina strikes the city, we wonder if he's survived OK.

Train conductors vary greatly; there are sticklers for the rules and some real comedians leading to hilarious announcements on the train. On the *Pioneer* (Seattle to Salt Lake City) in deepest Oregon, our conductor announces an upcoming stop *'hi folks, today we are making a stop at Baker for passengers, this is very unusual because normally we just put the mail pouch out to scoop up passengers who haven't told us they're joining. This is Baker, B-a-a-a-ker!'*

In 1991 on the *Coast Starlight* (LA to Seattle) approaching Olympia, Washington, we passengers are being entertained by the conductor running a *trivial pursuit* game from his cabin. He has a good line in quick witted humour and on passing a golf course here, tells how it was destroyed by a coating of ash from the 1980 Mount St Helen's volcanic eruption; fresh grass has grown since and now *'it's the only eighteen ashhole golf course in the USA'*. On the 1981 trip on the *Broadway Limited* when we could have done with information as the train is becalmed for eight hours at Monroeville, Pennsylvania, there is none (chap. 15). The height of cynicism is reached on the *Lake Shore Limited* (Chicago to Boston) on leaving Albany. The New York portion has left and the Boston portion leaves ten minutes later; it heads south instead of east, the conductor says not to be alarmed: *'we are following the New York route for a few miles, reversing a few miles, then reversing again to take the Boston and Albany, this is due to the stupidity of Conrail management who cut off the direct line!'*

Right: each San Francisco Cable Car has a multi-task brakesman, charged with the difficult business of controlling speed through brake and rack rail and revenue protection This one stands over the exit at the terminus: *'ladies and gentlemen, examine your consciences, it ain't too late to pay!'* After menacing the fare dodgers, the brakesman manually turns the Car at Fishermans Wharf (author)

Interesting travel companions

Left: dress etiquette gets a reality check in a rather grand Colorado country hotel, built in *Hollywood Baronial* style in film-buff Paul's opinion. We decide to dress for dinner with jacket and tie to be served by a waiter in jeans and tee-shirt! (author)

One of the nicest features about travel in North America is that everyone talks to you; there is not the traditional British reserve. In train dining cars, it is policy to seat people with other people to encourage conversation. Casual conversation on trains, buses and ferries is common and ranges over more than the weather; in fact, weather rarely comes up.

Here are some interesting people I meet:

On the *Pioneer* (Seattle to Salt Lake City), a young lady joins at Pocatello, Idaho and tells me she is a elementary (primary) school teacher in a school with a high proportion of Native Americans, was attracted by the high salary and loves her job; she dislikes Idaho and Pocatello in particular for its lack of culture. Hailing from Maryland on the east coast, she has been brought up in a much different, more formal culture.

On the overnight *South West Limited* (Chicago to LA) west of Kansas City the train is pretty full and my friends and I can't sit together; I'm paired with a young lady who turns out a most interesting travelling companion. Her job in life is in researching two of the famous overland historic trails (the *Santa Fe* and *Oregon*). I learn a great deal about the appalling problems the pioneers had to contend with and the detrimental effects on the Native Americans and consequently, don't get much sleep.

On the *Empire Builder* (Chicago to Portland) over lunch in the diner passing through Montana, Peter and I strike up conversation with a young man on his way to join a group of oceanographers on a project at the far end of the Aleutian Islands, 2,000 miles west of mainland Alaska; we learn about the interesting work he is doing related to climate and ocean currents. Living near Chicago, he does this trip by train several times a year as he doesn't like flying.

Left: on the *Desert Wind* (Ogden to Los Angeles), the train is passing through the Mojave Desert west of Las Vegas. I look out of the window for signs of life, flora and fauna and am not disappointed. A fellow passenger is perplexed that I should find a desert interesting; I tell her '*I have never seen a desert before and am utterly fascinated*'. She is speechless and thinks I'm very odd! (author)

There's the conversation between Josiane and an old lady travelling overnight on the *Ocean* (Montreal to Halifax) to attend a funeral in Nova Scotia. Discovering she is French Canadian, conversation switches to French and I later find out why Josiane keeps saying '*oui*'; not because she can't get a word in edgeways, it's because she has difficulty in understanding the Canadian's archaic French and native accent!

Off-beat North America

On our first *Rio Grande* Silverton train trip in Colorado, I listen to a father and son in conversation as we spot, alongside the train, a lavishly dressed man on a horse, a lookalike of film star cowboy Roy Rogers:

Son: '*Hey Dad, look at that cowboy*'

Dad: '*That ain't a real cowboy son, that's a dood (sic) cowboy*'

Son: '*What's a real cowboy like, dad?*'

Dad: '*A real cowboy's mean and dirty and got s..t all over him, son.*'

Our 1981 trip includes a three-day journey from Detroit to Denver, stopping off at St Louis, Missouri and is to take us through two 'wacky' places. First through Michigan on Amtrak's *Wolverine*, we stop en route at Kalamazoo (subject of Glenn Miller's *I got a girl in Kalamazoo..zoo..zoo..zoo*) and the name of an office accounting system that predated *Filofax* and computerisation. A sign at the station exit announces *yes, there really is a Kalamazoo*!

Kalamazoo Train Sta (Jeremiah Cox)

Three days later and we alight from the *Southwest Limited* at 'one-horse town', Lamar, Colorado *(right)* with several hours wait for a bus to Denver. Our arrival has attracted attention as prior to boarding, a local press reporter arrives to interview *these people from England* (clearly not a common sight!); after correcting him of our nationalities (Welsh, Scottish and English) we hastily dispatch him as our bus is about to leave, and wonder what on earth he would have asked us.

Later still on our 1981 trip we are on Amtrak's *Desert Wind* (Ogden-Los Angeles) overnight and oblivious to the world until daylight in the desert at Caliente, Nevada (*caliente* is *heat* in Spanish) 100 miles north of Las Vegas where we arrive two hours later. It's quite something to stop at this iconic place, another thing entirely that there is just 20 minutes to look around whilst the train is serviced. The station is part of Vegas Plaza Hotel and we walk through the foyer to the main street which at 08.30 hrs is utterly deserted. We've done Las Vegas in 20 minutes!

Above: most people are sleeping off the night before at 08.30 hrs in Las Vegas (author)

Right: a once common feature in the USA is of passenger trains going down the centre of a main street and picking up passengers by the big shops; in 1988 it's still done in Lafayette, Indiana where Amtrak's *Cardinal* (New York-Cincinnati-Chicago) stops for passengers outside *Woolworths*! I recall the same happened in Oakland, California in 1978. The conductors are bemused by our interest in something that is, of course, routine to them! (author)

113

Chattanooga is another famous place named in a Glenn Miller song, the *Chattanooga Choo Choo* and it's a rare pleasure in 1982 to join a steam train headed there, a two-day round-trip excursion from Lexington, Kentucky. It has its moments when on arrival at the famous city, its 600 passengers are bussed with efficiency to the hotel accompanied by police outriders on motorcycles, sirens blaring! The train panders to rail enthusiasts though a majority of patrons are natives; a run-past is arranged for photography in deepest Tennessee so picture the scene: the train stops (first passenger train for 25 years), several hundred people detrain, it reverses a mile then charges forward in full fury. A pipe-smoking hill-billy type sitting on his verandah is watching this and when the train storms past, exclaims in a beautiful deep-south lilt *'well I guess I seen everythin now'* and we all fall about laughing!

Wacky road signs: the USA is literal and direct with highway and roadside signing. Pedestrian crossings marked WALK or DON'T WALK, highway slip roads with WRONG WAY or TURN BACK YOU ARE GOING THE WRONG WAY, to cite two examples. At Cincinnati, a dual carriageway has the WRONG WAY sign upside down due to a missing lug! I just wish I could have taken a picture but in days of roll film, my roll runs out at that moment! Finally, in Kentucky on my 1982 visit after the rail tour mentioned above, we rent a car to explore the rural backwaters. In an area exemplified by the film *Coal Miners Daughter*, a lot of towns look like they haven't changed since the 1930's of the film set; it really is a trip back in time. We stay in Cumberland where the motel owner tries to interest us in his sideline of selling porn books! This fascinating area where Hazard is the principal town of Harlan County, a coal-mining part of the State and has its own police force: *Hazard Police.* There is no link to the TV soap drama *The Dukes of Hazzard* and I chuckle

when I think of UK temporary road signs *'Police-Hazard'*. Nearby is a very beautiful rural area known as *Kingdom Come State Park*, appropriately linking to the title of this book.

Top: the *'Chattanooga choo-choo'* in Tennessee (author)

Above: 'direct' street signage (shutterstock)

Right: Kingdom Come State Park, Kentucky (author)

Super Service

There's no doubt a lot of Americans go out of their way to make a visitor's time memorable and here is a sample of some of the good service I receive.

In 1982, Peter, Paul and I have double trouble. On our first day in New England, we take a 'rent a wreck' car to save money and return it within the hour! Setting out from Springfield a second time, we are unable to find accommodation as it is the weekend of return to university and hotels are full. A hundred miles later, we sleep in the car at the back of a *Holiday Inn* in North Boston. Cold and tired, we emerge from our car and into the hotel for a wash and brush up and breakfast. Our server, a cheery woman, takes pity when she hears of our overnight stay and piles on extra breakfast items without charge.

For the first days of my American holiday with Josiane, we stay at the *Dana Inn & Resort* in San Diego, and are served leisurely breakfasts as colourful as they are good; what looks like a 'knickerbocker glory' turns out as mixed fresh fruit of many colours topped with cream in a tall glass, an instant 'hit' with Josiane. More impressive is the way that our meals are served with style and elegance by server Jim; I am jealous that Josiane has eyes for Jim! The same hotel also saves us money advising against car rental as the public transit is so good.

You may not think that cut-throat car rental would deliver that bit more in service but you would be wrong. Mostly, their people are courteous, nowhere more than in Phoenix in 1981 when we alight and board the same train three days apart at around 06.30 hrs. On day one, we arrange rental from the train station, they pick us up within ten minutes, sign formalities and off. On return, they give us an early call at our motel, we take the car to the office and at 06.00 hrs they take us to the train station!

Unsightly development

A distinctly unattractive feature of American life is un-sightly development even in pristine country, sometimes up to the boundaries of National Parks (where planning regulations stipulate 'no development'). Grand Teton and Yellowstone National Parks abut aptly named Jackson Hole, gaudy, trashy, consecutive neon signs trying to outdo each other in height, vulgarity and inanity. All around the town is pristine wilderness especially Yellowstone.

Right: with trashy Jackson Hole behind the camera, I can view the Grand Tetons in all their majesty (author)

Stockton in the Golden State is a city that reminds us that California is not all sunshine and glitter; a more depressing place we have yet to encounter. With some hours to wait for a bus connection to Sacramento, we walk to the city centre (sic) to get lunch and find a giant car park surrounded by down-at-heel shops with no sign of even a decent café or diner, so we get a takeaway and return to the station.

Carson City: Peter and I make a diversion on our trip east of the Sierra Nevada to see the State capital of Nevada which can be modestly described as underwhelming. Maybe we expect too much for a State that devotes much of its resources to support the biggest gambling centres in the western world.

Inspiring Development

I end this chapter on an upbeat note and that is to say that some of America's greatest railroad stations have been saved for the nation. Most are sold off for development and some are tastefully refurbished even as their purpose has changed; some, like the doyen of them all, Cincinnati Union Terminal even gets its passenger trains back: six Amtrak *Cardinals*' per week, three each way!

Top: Carson City, unimpressive approach to a State capital. This is as far as we go as there is nothing to attract us (author)

Above: Cincinnati Union Terminal, art deco masterpiece of the 1930's is fully restored at the time of our visit in 1982; the ceiling of its beautiful ice cream parlour! (author)

Left: some small stations have also been beautifully restored like Glendale in California (author)

Right: for some, beauty is in the eye of the beholder and here a resident of Talkeetna obviously has feeling for the beauty of his town. In the completely unregulated environment of the USA and particularly Alaska, there are worse places than this. At least the view from the town is to die for (Mount Denali, highest point in the Americas, is close by) (author)

116

13   America's Great Outdoors - 1

New England, Canyonlands, Colorado and California

One of the best things I like about North America is its infinite variety in all things and particularly in landscapes, flora and fauna. Perhaps its greatest strength is the great outdoors admirably instanced by the beauty of National Parks and Forests. The former are well known, especially Yellowstone and Yosemite.

California east of the Sierra Nevada is a revelation as this photo of Mono Lake demonstrates (author)

In my nine visits to the continent, I have visited ten national parks and many more national monuments and landscapes and will share experiences of some of them with my readers.

My journey will take the reader in this and the following chapter from the pristine beauty of the New England coast and countryside, through the searing desert and mountain landscapes of the western Rocky Mountain States, the wild and wonderful State of Alaska, a California of infinite variety, the incredible beauty of Yellowstone National Park and finally to Paradise (a real place in Mount Rainier National Park) and the Oregon Coast (another un-named 'paradise').

This is a lot though it merely scratches the surface of this wonderful continent. Read on and enjoy!

One of the most pleasant surprises in my travels around the United States is New England. I go twice, both of a weeks' duration in The Fall; the first with Peter and Paul is timed when the colours are at their best; eighteen years later with Josiane, The Fall is later, and we arrive before the colours are at their peak.

Acadia National Park, Maine (author)

Finding Acadia National Park tucked on an island in the north-east corner of Maine is serendipity; small and perfectly formed with coastal scenery to die for. It is on the south of curiously named Mount Desert Island that the Park is situated, and it has two peninsulas with prominent though not high peaks. There is a significant settlement at Bar Harbour, an idyllic fishing port. The journey to and from Acadia is along the picturesque Maine coast road. The capital, Augusta is a modest and attractive city and a good centre for exploration. The south of the state has more interesting places and one that stands out is Kennebunkport, an attractive seaside town which has presidential connections as a summer vacation home for the Bush family.

A converted Dutch barn: Vermont (author)

Whilst Maine's attractions are mainly on the coast, landlocked Vermont, one of the smallest states by population and land area, is a rural joy which once hosted a large textile industry, now greatly diminished. Outside the textile towns are very attractive villages, becoming more so in The Fall. The Green Mountains are very scenic and agricultural with many colourful farm buildings and covered bridges, a unique feature of the State. The beauty of the area extends south and east into New Hampshire, very post-industrial (textiles again) with a substantial agricultural presence and a heavily populated coastal strip. Most towns and villages are noted for their beautiful white churches with colonnades and slender spires which makes driving through the area a pleasure.

Parts of the state are quite mountainous as the Green Mountains extend south from Vermont. Mount Monadnock stands in splendid isolation and gives its name to a geographical feature *Monadnock* meaning an outlying peak of a larger range. Not far from here and close to State capital Concord, is the university town

of Keene which has a beautiful and select suburb called Swanzee (sic), of particular interest to us as we live in Swansea. Local enquiries fail to establish a connection though I'm sure there is one.

A particular interest of mine is of course transport and railways in particular. New England is not busy with passenger trains though there is a

Mount Monadnock, New Hampshire (author)

small basic network which has expanded in the 22-year period of my American visits bringing Amtrak to Rutland, Vermont and Portland, Maine added to the one route between New York and Montreal through Vermont. The freight network is sparse and much of its former industrial traffic gone, though there are some attractive routes extant. In the mountains of New Hampshire, two routes cross, protected by America's last *highball* signal at Whitefield. When the ball is at its highest it is the signal for the train to proceed; and has given the name 'highball' in general as a sign for getting things moving.

Above: the last USA *highball* signal at Whitefield, New Hampshire. I'm lucky to see the only Maine Central train of the day heading towards Portland, Maine (author)

Right: Vermont is renowned for the outstanding beauty of a group of villages in the Green Mountain area of the State. The white painted houses and churches also in white with slender spires is a recurring feature, enhanced as in this picture by vivid Fall colours. This is the village of Grafton, one of three adjacent communities (author)

In complete contrast to elsewhere in the USA are the amazing landscapes to be found in the western States of Arizona, Colorado, New Mexico and Utah. Sometimes bizarre, they are formed by the forces of wind and water. The best known and most impressive is of course the Grand Canyon but there are others including Monument Valley and Arches National Park and the less dramatic mountains of Colorado.

Right: evening shadows lengthen on the south rim of the Grand Canyon (author)

Below: the iconic Saguaro Cactus is profuse in the desert around Phoenix (author)

The Grand Canyon is probably the best known and I have visited twice. The journey from the railhead at Flagstaff is over the high plains; on arrival I get a jaw-dropping sensation, struggling to take in its vastness. On the second visit which extends into evening, there are further sensational views as the sun goes down, the shadows lengthen, and colours become more vivid. There is something therapeutic in taking in the enormity of natural features, a feeling I get visiting other iconic sites in the West.

Arizona is a great State to travel through on the train and to see its fine topographical features, among them the *Petrified Forest* and vast areas of desert. Our road journey from Phoenix follows a route through the lesser known Oak Creek Canyon, whose features are on a much smaller scale. On arriving back from the Grand Canyon at Phoenix, Peter and I walk into the desert close to the city, where the amazing Saguaro Cacti are seen in profusion. We carefully make our way looking out for snakes and other hazards and are rewarded with striking photographs. It is interesting to see small and colourful flowers grow and birds' nests in the thick stems! Evening temperature is 100° F.

Although Arizona has wonderful landscapes, I find those in New Mexico and Colorado are even better and they are among my favourite States. Having travelled through them by train several times, I find it necessary to rent a car to be able to see the vast landscapes well off the beaten track.

My first visit to Colorado is in 1978 when I have a short stopover at Denver and tour the Rocky Mountain Park and surrounding area by car with Paul before heading west to California. Highlights include the historic town of Georgetown where its unique narrow-gauge railway is being restored, then over the 11,000 ft Berthoud Pass on a partly unpaved road (where we get our first sight of beavers at work) and the Colorado Railroad Museum at Golden with a fine collection of rolling stock from the D&RGW, Rio Grande Southern and other narrow-gauge lines.

Above: historic Georgetown, Colorado (author)

Below: an authentic Wild West Town, Gunnison, Colorado (author)

Two years later, we come with a plan to visit the famous narrow gauge Silverton line of the D&RGW, beautifully restored. It is a long drive to Durango which we make over two days finding out a lot about Colorado in the process. En route is the attractive city of Colorado Springs followed by wackily named Cripple Creek with its little tourist railway, later the *Manitou and Pikes Peak* cog railway and finally a highly scenic descent to the Alamosa Valley with a distant view of the San Juan Mountains.

The aptly named Buena Vista where we stay has wonderful views. It is on the original D&RGW main line between Pueblo and Glenwood Springs, sadly now a very minor route. From here, we take the famous Monarch Pass, through Gunnison, an old time Wild West town where we lunch at a saloon bar with slatted swinging doors - authentic stuff - and on to Silverton and Durango.

121

At Durango is another of my Colorado icons, the Silverton Line of the former Denver & Rio Grande narrow-gauge network which spanned much of the state in the Rocky Mountains. We travel the line (chap.18) and on return to Durango, go on by car through Silverton on a very different route to that of the railway and over the *Million Dollar Highway* to Ouray, named due to the vast expense in building it to open up the mining towns to road transport (hastening the end of the D&GRW!). We stay in Redstone at a grand hotel and next day's journey is via the resort of Glenwood Springs and the route of the *Rio Grande Zephyr* (chap.17) through canyons and Winter Park (a major skiing area, one of Colorado's modern attractions) on to Denver.

It is to be another twelve years before I visit these western USA States, mostly in Colorado and New Mexico also taking in Arizona and Utah. Follow us on our 1993 trip starting from El Paso, Texas. Heading north by car, we cross into New Mexico and stay in Las Cruces, a fascinating town with adobe style buildings. We eat *al fresco* and order a chilli-based meal; I ask the server the difference between green and red rellenos: *'well sir, the green are really hot, the red will blow your brains out!'* I opt for the green. It is a long haul north of over 300 miles to the night's destination of Farmington. On the way, intrigued by a place on the map named 'Truth or Consequences' thinking maybe it's derived from the words of a hell-fire preacher in the old days, so we call to investigate. Over coffee, I ask the server why it is named thus and her reply is unbelievable: *'it's after a popular NBC Radio quiz show in 1950 when the town was invited to gain national fame if they agreed to name it after the show, so they did!'* So why do people go there? *'Well you're here same as many others!'* It brings trade and money, very American; its previous name was Hot Springs.

Mittens and Merrick Buttes, Monument Valley, New Mexico (author)

Near Albuquerque, we briefly join the interstate highway before turning north on a secondary road through the hills for an evening arrival in Farmington. We're pretty tired checking into the Anasazi Inn, (the *Anasazi* was an ancient tribe wiped out due to climate change hundreds of years ago). After a meal, we summon the energy to travel 25 miles to Four Corners, conjunction of the states of Utah, Colorado, Arizona and New Mexico where an incredible natural landmark, Ship Rock appears like a ship in an empty landscape. Nearby is a very unpleasant man-made feature, the Four Corners, Lignite (dirty coal) burning power station whose pollution is so intense it can be seen from space.

Our itinerary continues next day heading into Arizona where the land around is lightly populated and mostly scrub. There are several Native American reservations for Navajo and Hopi tribes though we see little evidence of settlements until we turn to take the road north heading to Monument Valley.

The road leads to a plateau from where we can see a whole panorama of mesas and buttes which takes our breath away; this road is seemingly endless through a valley with more buttes randomly located all over this surreal landscape. We make a side trip to the visitor centre for refreshment and buy postcards and stamps. It's in the Navajo Reservation and I'm intrigued with their methods to extract cash from the white man, presumably as retribution for past injustices against their nation; nowhere else am I charged double face value for stamps, but there's no choice; I pay and marvel at their business sense, even if it seems like extortion.

Now in Utah, we see another incredible rock sculpture, appropriately named *Mexican Hat* which we stop at briefly before continuing through a land of more natural wonders to Monticello, where we stay. Our Canyonlands adventure is not yet over, and we are off next morning to Arches National Park near biblical-sounding Moab. The rock sculptures are formed from wind and rain erosion into amazing shapes, many of which resemble arches; we spend a few hours exploring these natural wonders Retracing our route to Moab, I notice a railroad in the canyon below, a branch from

Right: *Mexican Hat*, the amazing rock formation resembling a sombrero, is one of several bizarre rock formations (both photographs: author)

Left: the sheer variety of rock formations never ceases to amaze: Arches National Park is daddy of them all with lots of arches formed from erosion over millennia

Thompson on the D&RGW line to a potash mine. We travel into Colorado and New Mexico, ride the Cumbres & Toltec train (chap. 17), stay in Santa Fe (chap. 14) and to Albuquerque where we pick up our *Southwest Chief* to Chicago. There's not a lot to say about this city though we see *Route 66*, the highway made famous in Steinbeck's book *The Grapes of Wrath*.

In 1998, I'm back in Colorado with Josiane and show her this fantastic state as well as New Mexico on her first USA holiday. Arriving at Grand Junction on the *California Zephyr*, we rent a car and our first two nights are in Telluride. Once an important mining town, it rose to prominence on gold and silver prospecting; its last mine closed in 1978 and the town takes on a new role as a premier ski resort. The first day there is also my birthday and Josiane has planned a celebration meal in the evening. After looking round the town, we head out to the iconic Lizard Head mountain and on return, go to the old station for my birthday meal and some good local craft beer. They show us to the basement with no views, so we walk out and look for a better place which specialises in beef so we each have a nice rib-eye steak and enjoy it thoroughly.

Telluride's main street, the town almost completely hemmed in by mountains (author)

We leave the town heading north to Ridgeway then on the *Million Dollar Highway* to Silverton; having travelled 72 miles we are just 5 miles from Telluride as a high-flying crow flies! At Silverton, I look in on the narrow-gauge terminus which is very busy with four trains. Continuing, we pass through Durango, though not without difficulty; on approach the town, there is a violent storm and before we know it, a flash flood comes at us from the hill on the right, so this is not the time to stop for lunch! We stop at a diner in Ignacio then off to Pagosa Springs, a pleasant, former spa town and check into a guest house run by a German lady who serves us a Bavarian style dinner.

We take the road south through Chama where I take a brief look over the Cumbres & Toltec RR station; the day's train has gone and the hotel where I stayed in 1993 is closed. Next stop is Santa Fe; we stay two nights and Josiane takes an instant delight in this beautiful city, capital of New Mexico (chap. 14) and we have a whole day to savour its atmosphere. The journey into Colorado is along one of the most scenic

roads in the State. It follows the course of the *Chilli Line*, an outpost of the Rio Grande from Antonito to Santa Fe, closed in 1941, with one train a month in its final years. At Tres Piedras, in the middle of nowhere, a dilapidated water tower (*left*) a silent sentinel to a lost age!

As the road is very lightly trafficked, we are able to take in the fine scenery from the car. To the west is mysterious Los Alamos, a nuclear research establishment, still extant, where the first atomic bombs were conceived and tested. To the east a most incredible big sky effect reaches out to the beautifully named Sangre de Cristo Mountains. Some hours later we are in Colorado at the Native American settlement of Antonito, eastern terminus of Cumbres & Toltec Railroad. We stop here not so much for me to view the railway but for Josiane to browse the incredible array of exquisite Native American jewellery.

A striking vista across to the Sangre de Cristo Mountains in New Mexico (author)

The road to Antonito and beyond is on a plateau and runs dead straight for 50 miles before dropping down to Mineral Hot Springs, where we spot an amazing sight as at least 30 RV's the size of buses, are in convoy coming from the west. Fortunately, we reach the junction before they do and have a clear run to Salida, our destination for the night. Just before is Poncha Springs (a former railway junction) where the Jackson Hotel by the roadside turns out to be a museum with restaurant (*photograph below left*).

We go on to Salida, check into a motel and travel back to Poncha Springs for a meal. The upstairs rooms are devoted to Wild West characters and actors reputed to have stayed there. A young lady shows us round and rooms are variously Clint Eastwood, Billy the Kid, John Wayne, Jesse James and others. At the latter's room, Josiane asks our guide a question, like a bolt from the blue: '*did cowboys wear their boots to bed?*' Quick as a flash, she replies: '*not only did Jesse James wear his boots, when 'they' came to get him, he had a suit of clothes and ready saddled horse waiting outside, jumps through the window, on to his horse and away.*' I am speechless! It's an interesting experience if a bit hyped (but that's the American style), so we have a meal and laugh about it. Back at the motel, to complete the theme we watch two back-to-back *Westerns* starring Clint Eastwood!

We leave Salida via the impressive Monarch Pass, Tomichi Valley and Gunnison. From here is more scenic though some is man-made as the Blue Mesa reservoir was created in the 1960's completely obliterating the D&RGW's arguably most scenic and incredible route through the Black Canyon, closed 1948.

Soon after, we get to a lookout point above the Canyon which is very deep and narrow with sheer walls on either side. Josiane won't risk looking over though I do and have difficulty comprehending that a narrow gauge railway could have been constructed along the valley floor. Our next stop is Cimarron where we patronise a roadside diner and enjoy a Pecan Pie à *la mode* (with ice cream) and coffee. At Montrose, we turn on to US 50 for a straightforward run over the final 60 miles to Grand Junction.

Above: the idyllic Blue Mesa reservoir at the head of the Black Canyon of the Gunnison (author)

Below: the very deep Black Canyon; it's hard to imagine trains once ran alongside the river below (author)

The journey from Grand Junction on the *California Zephyr* to Denver completes our scenic extravaganza as we travel through the most attractive part of its route through the deep canyons, river and mountains (Chap. 17), though unforeseen delays make us two hours late at Denver. We call the hotel and request a courtesy car and ten minutes later a gleaming white *Lincoln Continental* arrives with a very courteous chauffeur; he takes our luggage to the room and offers to take us to the city for shopping in the morning. Our room and hotel is sumptuous and I check our payment schedule to find to great relief it's under $100 a night. On our final day we look around Denver and the hotel puts the chauffeur at our disposal to take us to the main shopping mall.

We are to return to the UK next day after another absolutely memorable holiday.

California is another State full of superlatives. Known as the wealthiest of all American States, it is not so well known for its wealth of landscapes and natural features. There are five National Parks within its boundaries and I've visited or passed through four of them. The real surprise is a hidden California east of the Sierra Nevada, abutting the State of Nevada and its range of amazing scenery and features, including Death Valley. I visit the State four times and still have much to see. First is in 1978 when I stay a few nights in Daly City, a suburb of San Francisco with friends of Paul. It's a wonderful introduction in one of its most 'off-beat' and beautiful cities (chap. 14). Paul and I then travel the scenic coastal railway route to Los Angeles and spend a night and day there visiting Universal Studios and a downtown Mexican market before heading east to Arizona, the Grand Canyon and more. It is enough to start changing my mind as I increasingly warm to California.

My next visit to the State is in 1981 (with Paul and Peter), arriving on a newly introduced Amtrak train, the *Desert Wind* from Ogden, Utah to Los Angeles. From there, we take the *San Diegan* most of the way along the Californian coast to Del Mar (*by the sea*), returning next day to LA and on overnight to Phoenix. The year I really start to appreciate this State is 1991 when I travel with Peter to San Francisco and Sacramento to visit the *Sacramento Rail Fair*, a colourful extravaganza of railway history and rolling stock. We have a day and a half here as there is so much to see and do, with a very fine Pageant and colourful displays of vintage steam and diesel locomotives and rolling stock.

Above: The beautiful *Bridal Veil Falls* in Yosemite National Park (author)

Right: The Southern Pacific *Daylight* locomotive is one of the star exhibits at the Sacramento Rail Fair Pageant (author)

Sacramento is a lively and gracious city with wide tree-lined streets, great restaurants and a tram network. We rent a car and spend the next eight days exploring the area north of here and later, 'hidden' California east of the Sierra Nevada. First to the Napa Valley, California's prolific wine producing area, our motivation, the tourist *Napa Valley Wine Train* thwarted as it's an expensive, upmarket operation beyond reach of our limited budget. We enjoy the trip around the area and return to Sacramento.

The following day, as we set out on our five-day tour east of the Sierra Nevada, learn that two giant Union Pacific steam locomotives are heading a 22-coach special train from Sacramento back to their base in Cheyenne, Wyoming via the former Western Pacific route through the Fraser River Canyon.

The steam special storms up the hill at Oroville, California (author)

It promises to be quite a day and initially, we drive to Oroville where the railway climbs steeply on a switchback and find hundreds of other photographers already there, at least confirming it as a good location, though there is trouble ahead. It is raining and it's not supposed to in California in May! Of more concern is a signal failure so we have to wait it out in the rain. After several hours, a long Union Pacific freight train passes and it seems the special isn't far behind. When it appears, the sight of two giant steam locomotives, a diesel and 22 yellow UP coaches blasting up the incline makes the wait worthwhile!

There is a mad scramble to get to the car on the road and pace the train; Peter is driving and remarkably positions us right opposite it in the canyon below, so I am charged with taking photos for both of us. At Nevada City, the road veers away from the railway, the chase is over and we head towards the Donner Pass and Truckee staying the night in a motel opposite the train station. At breakfast, from our window seat we watch a procession of Southern Pacific freight trains go past.

The next stage of our journey is south and the road fringes Lake Tahoe; on this side of the lake we are still in California. We soon cross into Nevada, a state known for its loose laws on gambling, and out of curiosity, head to the State Capital, Carson City which unlike other small Capitals, is underwhelming.

The state line is soon crossed and we remain in California from then on. It turns out to be a journey of great natural beauty, with the omnipresent Sierra Nevada on our right. The first natural wonder is Mono Lake, with its huge columns of 'tufa'; covering an area of 76 square miles and three-quarters of a million years old, the lake is very alkaline and the tufa is formed from a build-up of limestone.

The amazing Tufa columns on Mono Lake, California (author)

Further on is Mammoth Lakes Recreation Area which, in addition to its natural wonders, is a ski resort in winter. In late afternoon, we reach Independence and check in to a motel, only to discover the sole place to eat out is a *Subway* and it's a 25-mile journey to the nearest restaurant in Lone Pine. We make the trip and enjoy an excellent meal in the shadow of Mount Whitney (at 4,418 feet, highest point of the Sierra).

The next day is full of anticipation for what is to be a high spot of our holiday, Death Valley National Park. It is another of the USA's stunning parks, unique really, covering a much larger area than we anticipated. Leaving the main highway by the dry Owens Lake and climbing steadily to a high point (Towne Pass 1513 feet), then down through Stovepipe Wells to aptly-named Furnace Creek, close to the lowest point in the USA. Here we see the sign for sea level which demonstrates that the area beyond is below that.

Death Valley National Park, California, lowest point in the USA (author)

The landscape has a strange beauty in its aridity and in a small oasis known as Furnace Creek, there is a hotel which has to close in July and August as it's simply too hot! Whilst the lowest point covers an extensive area, most of the surrounding area is hilly, even mountainous, with some weird and wonderful natural sculptures and features, most unusual being Zabriskie Point. We retrace our route via Panamint Springs and the beautiful Panamint Valley to the small town of Ridgecrest, where we stay the night. This place abuts China Lake, a ghastly incursion of a military base in the midst of pristine territory.

Next day is through well-wooded countryside with lush pastureland, much like we see back home, then a picturesque journey through the giant redwood forests of Sequoia and Kings Canyon National Parks with stunning mountain scenery to Fresno, largest city of the San Joaquin Valley and stay the night. There is nothing to keep us here and we have an appointment with a steam train! Southern Pacific 4449 is hauling a train from Sacramento to San Jose and back which we hope to see on its return at Oakland, except we have no idea how busy the freeways of California can be and gridlock slows progress. The train has left Oakland, so we press on to Carquinez Strait in the hope of heading it off; we see the railway crossing the Martinez bridge and the presence of a large crowd of photographers suggests the train hasn't yet arrived, so we set up a good viewpoint and are rewarded by superb photographs.

The Southern Pacific *Daylight* special train after crossing Carquinez Strait (author)

We head back to Sacramento, turn in the car and back to our motel for one more night. That evening we go to the station where 4449 is resting and are invited on to the footplate, where I discover the engineer and fireman are volunteers with certificates permitting them to drive nominated routes. Shortly after, the engineer's shift is over, and he turns a key to shut down; it's an oil burning locomotive!

The next day is a bus/train/bus trip from Sacramento to Santa Barbara via Stockton and Bakersfield on Amtrak's *San Joaquin* through the rich and fertile Central Valley. At Bakersfield are connecting buses to destinations from Las Vegas to Santa Barbara; the latter is ours and arrival is late afternoon, giving time to explore this beautiful city. Our final day in California is aboard the *Coast Starlight* to Seattle.

In 1998, I make my final visit to California with Josiane. It is her first visit to the United States and California is a great place to start. We fly in via San Francisco, connect to San Diego and have a reservation at the Dana Inn & Marina in Mission Bay. The hotel is well appointed with a fine restaurant, pool, spa and use of a marina adjacent to Mission Bay where boats can be rented. We have leisurely breakfasts, as colourful as they are good. Public transport is good in San Diego including a bus service from our hotel to the city centre, and an extensive light rail system. The next day we get the bus to the city and buy a two-day transport pass. It is a thoroughly modern city with a fine historic core, the Gaslamp Quarter containing historic buildings including the original Mission and on this day an exhibition of classic American cars from the 1940's and 50's. The light rail system circumnavigates the old centre and radially to the suburbs on three routes. The Blue Route runs for 28 miles to San Ysidro at the Mexican border and our passes allow travel at no extra cost; we decide to go next day. We visit the Embarcadero, a waterfront area with a maritime museum and a collection of sailing ships, steamboats and ferries. The evening is spent in the old city; after dinner, we are surprised to find, despite its great wealth, San Diego has a substantial homeless problem as countless, mainly young, people are sleeping rough on the steps of City Hall.

A colourful street market in San Diego (author)

We are able to relax in our 'resort' hotel and one of its facilities is free boat hire; the choice is between an outboard-motor dinghy or an aqua scooter, capable of higher speeds. Having dreamt the previous night about seeing *'Davy Jones' locker'* at the bottom of the lake, I opt for the former, safer, boat and we have a great morning's fun on the water. Seeing the way some of the young men are behaving on their aqua scooters (there are no mandatory speed limits), I feel vindicated by my choice. Looking across the lake, I see the main railway line and get my first introduction to the newly-introduced *Coaster* commuter trains.

The next day is our light rail trip on the Blue Line (in a bright red tram) to San Ysidro along the coast with arrival there about an hour later.

From Californian sublime……   ……to Mexican cor blimey! (author)

We transfer from our stylish modern tram to a ramshackle *Mexicoach* bus takes us on a one-mile, $1 journey over the border to Tijuana; in five minutes from one of the world's highest GDP's to one of the lowest.

Tijuana is a chaotic and colourful city and an interesting look into Mexican life (author)

The city is exotic and very busy with gaudily-coloured buildings, street markets and a chaotic air. We love the markets but are wary of cafés which are not the cleanest. We return in late afternoon which is less easy than coming; there are checks of all vehicles at the border and the bus doesn't get priority and moves slowly, so the driver suggests walking to avoid a long delay. The return tram ride is uneventful and such a contrast to what we have witnessed over the border.

Since my trips in California in earlier years, a revolution has happened with the train services; San Diego has its *Coaster* commuter service and an extensive light rail system, Los Angeles, heavy and light rail systems and the number of Amtrak *Pacific Surfliner* trains up from 6 to 11 trips per day; we take the mid-day *Surfliner* to Santa Barbara.

We are to spend the next week in San Francisco and our stay is described in more detail in chapter 14, though our excursion to Yosemite is described below.

In planning our day to Yosemite National Park, we discover that an all-inclusive coach tour costs $100 each but our Amtrak pass covers both train and bus connection to Yosemite, a free day out! We are up early, a downside to our 'free' trip and get a bus to the *San Joaquin* at Emeryville; our train has double deck coaches with an *Amdinette* and we enjoy an appetising breakfast. The journey is to Merced in the San Joaquin Valley, nearest station to Yosemite; a connecting bus is waiting for the 2½ hour journey to the Park. The route climbs, twisting and turning in a deeply wooded valley and at Yosemite, is quite high up. The terminus at Yosemite Village is an attractive settlement with no commercial development in the valley of the Merced River. The main attractions, *Half Dome* and *Bridal Veil Falls* are within walking distance and we have three hours in which to enjoy it. The scenery of the valley and its physical features are stunning and we watch spellbound as climbers tackle Half Dome.

Above: the spectacular *Half Dome*, one of Yosemite's best features (author)

Right: our *San Joaquin* train between Emeryville and Merced is run by Amtrak under contract to CalTrain. This arrangement has massively improved train services in the State of California (author)

It's a three-hour journey back to San Francisco and our train from Merced is delayed by a freight train, but it's been a great day!

In this second part, I take the reader through the amazing State of Alaska which I have visited twice, followed by a trip along the highly scenic west coast in Oregon, a wild and wonderful journey. Though I find the entire coastline a paradise, it is some days later that I find the real Paradise, the name given to an area of Mount Rainier National Park where its lodge and visitor centre is situated.

So this is PARADISE! the Lodge and Visitor Centre in Mount Rainier National Park (author)

Finally, to Yellowstone National Park, the most famous of all the Parks, the first such to be established in the USA (1872) and probably in the World.

Gateway to adventure: the south west entrance to Yellowstone Park (author)

Above: Juneau

Below: Mark Air flight to Fairbanks

(both photos by the author)

For years, Alaska has been in the too difficult category and when Peter and I decide to go in 1988, we opt for a short visit in case it disappoints. How wrong we are and filled with regrets about having just three whole days there. It serves to strengthen our resolve to return, which we do three years later. It's a State like no other I have visited for its wonderful mountains, rivers, glaciers and other natural features in abundance. I make two visits, both accompanied by Peter; first in 1988 when we take the incredible train journey from Fairbanks to Anchorage (chap.16).

Independent travel to Alaska is not for the faint hearted; nevertheless, we choose Friday 13 May 1988 for our trans-Atlantic flight in anticipation it will be lightly loaded. We are not disappointed; our *Wardair* DC10 from Gatwick to Vancouver is less than half full. It is a ten-hour journey with a stop at Edmonton, arriving early evening in Vancouver for transfer to the bus terminal for the *Greyhound* and a four-hour journey to Seattle. Next day to Seattle-Tacoma Airport and we're booked on the *Northwest* flight to Anchorage, Alaska; only we're not! There has been overbooking and an airline official offers cash for us to take a later flight. It is declined as we have an important connection at Anchorage for the onward flight to Fairbanks. This is common, a deliberate policy to get high load factors and keep down fares, but ours are not cheap at $200! Soon after, seats are found, and we enjoy superb views of the British Columbia and Alaska coastline. Arrival at Anchorage is dramatic; the plane flies in from the south above *Turnagain Arm* toward a sheer cliff on top of which is the airport - a tad scary. I get a feeling of sheer elation that I felt on my first time to the USA in 1978!

There is over two hours to wait for our connection, the 17.00 hrs to Barrow on the north coast of Alaska. It is a Boeing 737 hybrid (passenger/cargo) operated by local company *Mark Air*; journey time to Fairbanks 55 minutes in contrast to the train schedule of 10½ hours! The airport there is about twenty miles out of town and our pre-booked motel, the exotically named *Klondyke Inn*, is roughly halfway. Its appearance is entirely consistent with its name, and it offers both accommodation and catering.

The Klondyke Inn, Fairbanks' Premier Motel! (author)

Appearances are deceptive and it has a fine steak house; the waitress takes our order and tells us she once served on the trains and that they always run late. The cooking range is circular surrounded by a serving counter though we sit at normally arranged tables. The chef is cooking lots of steaks and suddenly there's a sheet of flame and badly charred meat. Nonchalantly, he gathers up the ruined steaks, bins them, cleans up, takes fresh steaks from the fridge and resumes cooking - all without a word, unbelievable!

We leave early next morning and take a taxi into Fairbanks; our train, the *Aurora*, is formed of four railcars of 1962 vintage and will take twelve hours for the highly scenic journey to Anchorage (chap. 16). It is apt to add at this point that nearly everything about this journey and Alaska in general is unexpected, a new dimension on life which is much more informal than we are used to. As the journey progresses, so does our resolve to come back some day and see more of this amazing State. One place on the route, Wasilla, is to come into prominence years later as the home of Sarah Palin, Governor of Alaska and vice-presidential hopeful (which god forbade!); her lifestyle shocked a lot of people but not me as it is entirely consistent with what I see on this and my later trip. We don't quite see the summit of Denali, highest point in North America, due to persistent high cloud. An annoyance when we check into a city centre hotel is a 50% price increase the following night (start of summer season) so we opt for one night and look for an alternative.

In the morning we realise what a large place Anchorage is, spread over a vast area but having a population of c.250,000; yet it is not the state capital, that title belonging to much smaller Juneau further south. We pick up a rental car and look for accommodation which is the *Puffin Inn*, near the airport - room only - but across the road is *Gwenny's Kitchen*, a diner doing fabulous breakfasts and dinners.

We head south on a road that runs alongside *Turnagain Arm*, a long sea inlet named by Captain Cook after sailing in search of the mythical northwest passage and turning back on finding it was not. It's a very scenic route to Girdwood, junction for rail and road with Seward line and branch to the port of Whittier through a massive mountain in a 2½ mile road/rail tunnel used only by road vehicles, rail freight and cruise trains.

Above: Alaska RR freight train at Girdwood

Below: a serene evening at Turnagain Arm

(both photos by the author)

As we take in the scene, an oil tanker train comes along and takes the line to Whittier. Returning to our car, we hear on the radio that the road back to Anchorage is blocked by a landslide. Another driver tells us to be patient as this is a common occurrence and will be fixed which it is in about half an hour. We drive past with some trepidation in case of another slide. On our final day in Alaska, we eat a massive breakfast in *Gwenny's*, return our car to the airport and take a mid-morning *Northwest* flight (without the hassle this time) for the four hour journey back to Sea-Tac airport.

In 1991 Peter and I are back in Alaska at the capital, Juneau, having arrived on the *Alaska Marine Highway* from Bellingham (chap. 11). I take up the story from Juneau.

We explore the city and its surrounding area. It is a land-locked place, impossible to reach other than by sea or air. It was a principal base for gold prospectors who had a really hard time getting to the gold fields, having to scale high mountains, many perishing in the attempt. In the city, they were drinking and gambling to excess and we see one of the notorious drinking dens, the *Red Dog Saloon* in historic downtown.

There is evidence of past Russian influence with an Orthodox Church and other artefacts and in the afternoon, enjoy a bus tour which takes us to the massive Mendenhall Glacier, one of the largest in the State. We arrive by sea and depart by air, exhausting all of the city's external travel options.

The flight with state carrier *Alaska Airlines* is two-hours with two intermediate stops, Yukutat and Valdez (the latter the site of a dramatic oil spill two years earlier which had devastating environmental impact). The view of the landscape from the air is breathtaking as we fly above the Wrangell St Elias National Recreation Area. On arrival at Anchorage, we stay at the *Puffin Inn* again, and arrange a car in which we plan to explore the area up to and including Denali National Park.

Next day, we head north of the city and stop over to explore some of the wild forest area near Eklutna; alert to the possibility of bears though thankfully don't encounter any. Returning to the car, we lunch at a roadside log cabin diner and continue the journey to Palmer and stay the night; the weather is cloudy with some light rain. The following day, we travel north to Talkeetna, famous as starting point for most of the expeditions to *Denali*, highest mountain in North America (20,250 feet). It's a sobering thought that fewer than half of climbers make the summit and a significant number need rescue; the weather precludes us seeing the mountain! Talkeetna has the look of a pioneer town and has a lot of charm. We travel on to Denali Park, and check into the *Princess Hotel* (owned by the cruise company).

It's another cloudy day but we go into the Park nonetheless. Access is strictly controlled and it's necessary to book seats on a bus tour to take us up its only internal road for 50 miles; buses are retired school vehicles with slatted seats, preparing us for a very basic day out. The journey is magical and we spot moose, elk and some grizzly bears. The road ends at a river basin surrounded by snow covered mountains and it's a great view. Beyond, access is allowed only by permit and limited to several thousand people a year. The Park is massive, about the size of Wales with just this one road and no resident population. We have a picnic lunch and enjoy the view before the return journey. On arrival, we see a demonstration of husky dogs sled racing; the centre has a large number of these dogs, a third of whom are used on each demonstration organised by the park rangers. It's fascinating to witness their enthusiasm as they set out on the run, even more so, the howls of disappointment from those left behind.

Above: Annahootz mountain range in Denali National Park (author)

Left: highlight of our visit is the dog-sled race near the Park's Visitor Centre. These dogs are in regular training for the massive annual event over hundreds of miles, known as the Iditarod Race (author)

Next day, we explore north of *Denali* and, as the sun has finally broken through, hope we finally get sight of the summit of this famous mountain. We take a side road heading towards the Yukon hoping to see more of ultra-remote Alaska but it's a rough ash surface and as we progress, becomes rutted and soft and realise just in time that a four-wheel drive is needed for such conditions. Back on the main road Mount Denali is in the distance and as we reach the crest of a hill at Cantwell, there it is in all its glory. Wow! At this point, it is over 50 miles away though it seems much closer; this is because it stands out against the surrounding mountains which are no higher than 8,000 feet.

Mount Denali, all 20,250 feet stands out from surrounding peaks; we are 50 miles away! (author)

Flush with success, we return to the hotel for dinner, during which time the staff have heard they are to be made redundant the next day; two cruise liners have collided in Whittier and cruising tourists' holidays have been terminated, so numbers at the hotel will drop catastrophically. Unsurprisingly, service is not exactly with a smile though the meal is good. Next day, we go to the train station to photograph the Alaska Railroad's tourist train; it is peak season, and the *Denali Star* runs daily with 12 coaches, double deck glass-roofed vehicles hauled by two locomotives.

After that, we head back to Anchorage; after an hour's driving on a long straight road, we spot a large animal crossing ahead; as we get closer, it's a black bear so is worth a photo or two. I wind down the window and as I get my camera ready, the bear advances and I hastily shut the window; this happens several times so my eventual shot has camera shake; then another car comes and frightens the bear back into the bushes.

Right: after several abortive attempts at a photograph, I resign myself to an out of focus result and title the shot 'Fuzzy Bear' (author)

The remainder of the journey is uneventful apart from noting the bizarre names of roadside features. A bridge over *Question Creek* is followed by *Answer Creek*; and then there is *Ship Creek*, the original name of Anchorage. We check into the *Puffin Inn* and dine at *Gwenny's Kitchen*. The chef offers his last two freshly caught wild salmon fillets, so we decide to have them, much to the annoyance of a couple on the next table; it's the finest salmon I've tasted!

On our final full day in Alaska, we decide to complete the railroad mileage by taking a train to the port of Seward, a wonderfully scenic journey in a railcar crossing three huge glaciers. We have a young student guide, Stephanie, who entertains us with some interesting facts, including that adjacent houses have hangars rather than garages as their owners get around by plane!

Above: end of the line, the railcar lays up at Seward for four hours before the return journey (author)

Below: a Sea Otter in Seward Bay swimming belly-up but without young (author)

Seward is a small town with a large port. It is also noted as being the last outpost in Alaska of Sea Otters, creatures which have a pouch on their belly for their young; they swim upside-down, so the young keep their bodies above water! There were once millions of these creatures, but Russian trappers hunted them for their fur, almost to extinction.

On 'going home' day, we are due to leave in afternoon on a direct British Airways flight to Heathrow, a Jumbo 747 en route from Japan to London which calls at Anchorage for refuelling. Thus we are not surprised then when a tidal wave of Japanese tourists descends on the concourse. After an hour, the plane reloads and we're off. I recall the difficult landing in 1988 and realise it's also a steep take off for a large plane with the mountains so close. When airborne, we see *Mount Denali* clearly even though it's 150 miles away; then it heads over the frozen north and the Arctic Ocean and during the night we are close to the North Pole. We land at Heathrow in the early morning ending a truly epic trip.

My first introduction to the Pacific north-west coast is in Seattle in 1980 though it's not until 1993 that I am to travel up the coast of Oregon. It is a most amazing, wild and picturesque coastline. Peter and I continue that year to Mount Rainier National Park in Washington where we find Paradise though I wonder whether we haven't already found it along the coast! Arriving at Seattle in 1978 from Vancouver, I already have a brief taste of the coast on the *Greyhound* bus though in that first year, Seattle is just a transit point and I don't even see the waterfront.

Left: the wild Oregon coastline at Netarts Bay (author)

Below: the Space Needle in Seattle (author)

Two years later, I am in Seattle again with Peter and Paul and we have a full day in the city. It is a most agreeable place buzzing with life and very prosperous. Some years earlier, it had hosted a World Trade Fair and the site is still there with many of its futuristic icons including the Space Needle serving as tourist attractions. Seattle is not on the Pacific coast but the Puget Sound, an arm of the ocean with the Olympic Peninsula on the far side. Eating out on the waterfront in the evening is sublime, watching ferries and other shipping going to and fro.

It is to be 13 years before Peter and I return to the Pacific Northwest arriving at Portland on the *Empire Builder* and renting a car for five scenically delightful days on the Oregon Coast and Mount Rainier National Park.

We join the coast highway at Newport, Oregon and travel over 150 miles to Aberdeen, Washington and are struck by its outstanding natural beauty. We stop off several miles later at Otter Crest, where there is an idyllic resort with cabins in the woodland above the sea.

Next day, we resume our journey on this outstanding route with every coastal view seemingly better than the last. There are lots of coves, bays, capes, pristine beaches and amazing rock formations, some as outliers from the coast. One of the finest sights is Nestucca Bay and this is where the highway 101 heads inland, so we take a minor road and stay close to the coast.

Top: Oregon Coast gem; the hidden cove at Otter Crest (author)

Above: two of many outlying rocks off the coast at Oceanside; a common coastal feature (author)

The succession of amazing beaches on this road is quite breathtaking and soon we reach the little port of Tillamook and the Port of Tillamook Bay Railroad, a freight and heritage line. We spot a freight train with a cargo of packaged timber heading east towards Portland.

We are told of an attractive area back on the coast which means heading out from here on a minor road to Cape Mearns and the attractive resort of Oceanside where arrival is in late afternoon. Here we find a hotel with individual chalets on a hill above the coast and check in for the night. We head to town for a meal, return to our chalet later and sit in the sunshine with a bottle of chilled white Oregon wine and watch the sun set over the Pacific...perfect! After this, can things get any better?

Wild and beautiful Cape Lookout, Oregon Coast (author)

Well, they certainly stayed as good when we continue on the main coast road and arrive at the small port city of Astoria. It is famous for its four-miles long bridge across the mouth of the Columbia River which we cross (some years later I recognise this bridge in the film *Kindergarten Cop* starring Arnold Schwarzenegger).

The other side of the river is Washington State and the Olympic peninsula, also known for its outstanding scenery. The road continues close to the coast and loses its dramatic qualities this far north, and when we reach Aberdeen, realise it will be too ambitious to circumnavigate the entire peninsula and still have time to visit the national park. The road veers away from the coast through unremarkable country to State capital Olympia where we stay the night. It is a pleasant place with a fine view east to the iconic Mount Rainier.

The next day, we plan to visit the Mount Rainier National Park and it is not far to the junction from *Interstate* Highway 5 to the National Park highway, later diverging on to a long, winding and steep road through dramatic scenery to arrival at Paradise, an entirely appropriate name given to this part of the National Park and its Lodge, where we stay and explore the idyllic area with a clear view of *Mount Rainier*. In the evening, we take a trip to the aptly named Reflection Lake where we have an excellent (and reflected) view of the snow-capped 14,400 foot mountain. I also reflect on the fact that it is twenty years since I discovered Hell on the beautiful Norwegian coast and it occurs to me that there is always the possibility of this paradise becoming hell if the mountain (an active volcano) blows its top.

The idyllic evening view of Reflection Lake, Mount Rainier National Park says we have reached Paradise! (author)

We enter the Park on the southern flank and leave Paradise heading east circumnavigating the mountain and getting further fine views of this fantastic peak. The road eventually takes us around the north of the Park and down into the industrial city of Tacoma where we check into a harbour-side motel for our final night before flying back to London next day.

A final look at Mount Rainier, seen from the dockside at the port of Tacoma (author)

Yellowstone is the first of the really great national parks I visit and highlight of my 1981 holiday with Peter and Paul. It is situated in northern Wyoming and to get there we take the train to Ogden in Utah then a car for the journey, mostly through Idaho. Join us as we leave Ogden; the route is via Brigham City (after Mormon pioneer, Brigham Young) and Idaho Falls in the south east corner of the State of Idaho, where we come to the majestic Snake River, one of the longest in the USA rising in Yellowstone park and feeding the Columbia River a thousand miles on. It is a tranquil scene and a great introduction to what is to come.

Majestic and serene: the mighty Snake River near Idaho Falls, Idaho (author)

From here it is very rural with a few small settlements, and we stay at an unmemorable one named Driggs. Soon after, we cross into Wyoming and the Grand Teton National Park, after a mountain range of the same name. The entrance is at aptly named Jackson Hole, a ghastly tourist honeypot in the middle of superb landscape. Here in sharp relief is the massive divide between national park and outside; Jackson's brashness assaults the senses with neon signs outdoing the other in height and vulgarity, trashy gift shops and motels; the aptness of the suffix *Hole* is clear! The gateway to the park leads to unspoiled countryside; zero tolerance to development within national park boundaries with strict measures to control it. Consequently, Parks are natural, pristine ecosystems. The Yellowstone Lake Lodge continues the theme, being built entirely of natural materials and a is joy to stay at for our two nights thereat.

The Lake Lodge has the most amazing view southwards over the lake and is well placed for excursions within the Park. Day one sees us at the *Old Faithful* geyser shooting over 100 feet into the air at regular intervals just over once an hour. Around are numerous ponds and creeks filled with sulphuric and other dangerous natural acids, which visitors are advised to keep well clear and warned not to put their hands in the water.

Left: the *Old Faithful* geyser shoots over 100 feet in the air at fairly regular intervals, usually one to one and a half hours apart. It is the largest attraction in the Yellowstone National Park (author)

Some of these features are very colourful with the combinations of rocks, soil and acids creating amazing effects. We are so fascinated by these natural wonders that the day goes quickly as we await further eruptions of *Old Faithful* and explore ever more weird and wonderful smoking pools of pure acid. A road leads from here to the Yellowstone River Canyon though we give this a miss intending to spend more time there on the second day.

We return to our lodgings and at the end of the day, explore the peaceful and bucolic Hayden Valley which amongst other attractions has a decent herd of bison, lots of elk and birds such as pelicans and great egrets which we don't see back home. There is interpretive information at the Lodge and park rangers are on hand to answer questions; there is little doubt of their strong commitment to their work though it seems they don't get paid very well. The next day we travel about ten miles to the amazing Grand Canyon of the Yellowstone, with its psychedelic range of colours; yellow, brown and orange variations in the strata and at its head the Lower and Upper Falls. We spend a lot of time photographing from various angles before returning to the lodge.

The Grand Canyon of the Yellowstone River and the magnificent Upper Falls (author)

We have seen a lot in two days though the area of the park is vast and there is insufficient time to explore further. Reluctantly, we retrace our route via the west bank of Yellowstone Lake to Jackson taking the road south to a small settlement in aptly named Alpine. We check into a motel/resort where accommodation is in individual chalets with superb views. Its owner is a portly regal lady who might well have been the actress Margaret Rutherford. She keeps a house consistent with her image including a gold leaf covered visitor book. Paul in a mischievous mood decides to sign himself in as *Lord Collenette of Kingston* (Paul lived in Kingston upon Hull at the time) and is convinced she will try in vain to locate the name in Burke's Peerage! Leaving aptly named Alpine we drive through scenery one could easily associate with its name, back to Ogden in Utah. We are to take the train from here to Los Angeles.

The serene and beautiful Hayden Valley, Yellowstone National Park (author)

On the north bank of Yellowstone Lake, I see my first bison close up (author)

15   My favourite American cities

New York Boston Chicago San Francisco Santa Fe Charleston

Most people build up misconceptions about countries and places they haven't visited, and I am no exception. My prior views of North America came from learning about the countries in my 'A Level' studies (mostly positive) and through news items and general views which seemed to be shared by many that it is not our sort of country. It isn't helped in my case that railways had a really bad time: the Pennsylvania Railroad crash in the 1960's, largest corporate failure in Wall Street's history; and the collapse of passenger trains resulting in the formation of Amtrak in 1971 seen as a means of managing the inevitable decline.

The cities are something else, seemingly ruined by the incursion of the motor car often becoming parking lots with shops rather than the other way round.

I learn very quickly that generally, North America doesn't live up to my prejudices and after the first visit in 1978, just try and stop me going again!

Even so, I have to admit ambivalence about America's cities, dismissive of New York, Chicago, Los Angeles and Miami but looking forward to seeing Boston and San Francisco and not knowing much about Charleston, Sacramento, San Diego and Sante Fe. All this counts for nothing in practise; nothing beats 'being there' in correcting or reinforcing misconceptions.

New York delights: Manhattan Island looking north from the Empire State Building (author)

My first contact with America is New York, though the first trip is in transit. On arrival, I'm apprehensive as the city's reputation goes before it and am expecting to witness violence. A disorderly arrival at JFK airport doesn't help though it's mainly positive from then on. I learn to be vigilant - being short-changed on a room service breakfast and Paul is relieved of cash from his pocket - but warm to the place as I find it is lively and colourful with masses of people out enjoying themselves. In later years I spend several days in the city and get to like its vibrancy and 'can do' attitude.

On this and subsequent visits, I am accompanied - except on the final day of my first trip - alone in the city - before a rendezvous with Paul. It is then that I feel vulnerable and imagine bad things can happen; they don't. First impressions count and my fear of violent attack diminishes when I see so many people acting out their lives normally. The hotel is fine apart from a room service incident on the first morning. I get a 'wow' feeling seeing the city in daylight and particularly the magnificence of Grand Central station. A few weeks later I have a phobia in Penn Station diner as I'm eyed by a man evidently under drug influence and convince myself he's going to pull a gun on me. I run short of cash on the taxi journey to the air terminal so bale out and walk a half-mile to reduce my outgoings.

Above: the Chrysler Building from the East River. It is probably the second most iconic building in New York after the Empire State (author)

Right: For 50 cents, we get the classic Manhattan view from the Staten Island Ferry. The twin towers on the left are to disappear exactly one year after my final visit (author)

I make use of Grand Central several times in subsequent years during which time it receives a massive makeover, restoring its original magnificence as one of the World's greatest stations. On each visit to the city, I progressively see the attractions starting with the Empire State Building and Staten Island Ferry, later Central Park and midtown Manhattan, building up a collection of photographs.

One of my best photographic efforts is with Peter when we discover a location to record Manhattan lighting up. It's not without its drama; Brooklyn Bridge has a central pedestrian walkway straddling the road with long lead up ramps each end from which there is no escape other than jumping off the bridge! When we finish, it is dark and there are few people about. Forearmed with cameras slung over our shoulders (as defence) we walk off the bridge past several suspicious looking characters who turn out to be harmless.

Left: the classic Manhattan skyline from Brooklyn Bridge, my final picture after a session lasting over a two-hour evening period. It is worth the wait even if we don't anticipate the dangerous situation we are putting ourselves in! (author)

Each time, I am building up a picture of the quirkiness of this city, its frenetic pace, the impatience of people and the *'Sylvester Stallone'* twang. Central Park can equal any in the variety of ways people are enjoying themselves; a man walking six Siamese cats on a lead, another standing on his head for a long period, another flat out on a bench, arms and legs in X shape, informal sports matches. One day, we arrive at 103rd Street on the Subway and, finding ourselves in Harlem with that 'oh s..t' moment, are greeted by a black resident *'welcome to the greatest city in the world'* and he didn't mean New York!

The longest time I spend in the city is in 2000 when I am with Josiane and we have four days. Methodically, we plan to walk from South Ferry to the top of Central Park over three days using the bus or subway to end or restart each day. That way, we see most of the city and what an experience it is! On day one, we take the Staten Island Ferry, the best value ride in America at 50 cents a round trip with views of the Statue of Liberty and south flank of Manhattan. We explore the Financial District, buying lunch at a takeaway salad bar which charges by weight; selecting expensive seafood with salad, keeps cost down and value up!

We don't visit the World Trade Centre as we've already done the Empire State. It is September 11 2000, one year to the day when these twin towers will be no more; a scary thought!

Wall Street is interesting, its fine gothic church overshadowed by sky-scrapers. There is a lot more of interest including a lively fish market on the East Side, a real surprise. *Chinatown* is a maze of small streets, restaurants and businesses with colourful signs in Chinese. We see the Woolworth Tower, among the earliest iconic New York buildings. Another ethnic neighbourhood is Little Italy, with its Italian-style businesses. Finally, elegant Greenwich Village, the arty heart of New York City with stylish houses and tree-lined boulevards. After enjoying this fascinating variety, it is time to return to our hotel, so we take the bus. The journey is interesting if only for another quirky feature of New York; a lack of social interaction between public service workers. At one stop, there is someone in a wheelchair so, with not a word, our driver gets out, operates the chair lift, gets the passenger on board and resumes the journey. Soon after, he is relieved by a colleague and the whole process is carried out without a word between drivers!

Wall Street, financial centre of the world, dwarfs its parish church! (author)

In the evening, we go to Times Square to soak up the neon-light filled atmosphere and dine in the Times Square Brewery, also a restaurant. Tables are arranged round a central core in which stands a huge copper brewing vat; steak and real ale is a winning combination which we enjoy! We take a leisurely walk to the hotel when Josiane finds her handbag is missing, so it's back to the restaurant but they have nothing handed in, so I assume she has been pickpocketed. Fortunately, there is no cash or cards in it but expensive cosmetics which need to be replaced. That prompts a visit to Macy's the next day.

Day two and we are to resume our walk through Manhattan at Greenwich Village but first we must go to Macy's on 34th Street close to the hotel. Reputed to be the World's largest department store, it certainly looks impressive though a bit old-fashioned. While Josiane is choosing a new handbag and cosmetics, I look around and note with interest that discounts on goods are given by the hour rather than the day or week. We

New York bus and iconic Yellow Cabs

take a bus to Greenwich Village and resume our walk uptown through Manhattan, first heading toward Times Square and 42nd Street mostly along the famous Broadway.

The street is unusual in running obliquely through the grid pattern for which I assume the reason is it must have been the earliest street in Manhattan which the grid grew around. We walk towards the East River to see the famous Chrysler Tower and the United Nations Building. From here it is a few blocks to chic Lexington Avenue where Josiane enjoys window shopping to see New York's latest fashions. By now we have seen most of high rise New York as there is more open space further uptown with Central Park dominating. The East River waterfront gives us a good view across to Queens and Brooklyn and a look back on Manhattan.

The East River from the Manhattan shore looking across to Brooklyn (author)

Day three and we take a short subway ride to 42nd Street and resume our northward walk towards Up-town, Central Park, and Harlem. Central Park is an absolute delight and noticeably cleaner and safer when I was here twenty years ago. As then, there are masses of people enjoying themselves with organised and unorganised events taking place all over the park. There is a rock concert taking place in an arena in Central Park with the famous singer, *Sting*. Even if we could afford it, there is no way we're ever going to get near the event; interesting that he's chosen the same day as us to be in New York! At the north end is the infamous suburb of Harlem which is much cleaned up and is now quite inviting. Within its boundaries, the largest cathedral in the world, St John the Divine has been over 100 years in the building and still incomplete. Though we look around, I can't say I find this cathedral remotely attractive.

We return to our hotel by Subway ending three wonderful days exploring this great city. It is only on this third day that I persuade Josiane that we should travel on the Subway and, though it is dimly lit and noisy, is more acceptable than its reputation would suggest. I have seen and travelled on its darker days twenty years earlier when it was still categorised as risky if not dangerous to travel. It is certainly noisy, dirty and graffiti-ridden though surprisingly efficient.

Graffiti, dirt, noise, crowds but exciting: the New York Subway (author)

Boston is the only US city I visit on my own in 1978 when Paul and I split up at Chicago; he travels to Newark, New Jersey for an interview with the son of inventor Thomas Edison and I opt to visit Boston. I certainly have a great day and a bit here to look around at this, probably America's most historic city. As well as looking at the city centre, the old and new State House, Boston Common and other iconic places, I take a tram to Cambridge, where world famous Harvard University is located and is most interesting. I find Boston's transit system functioning though ramshackle and because it has so much vintage rolling stock, a joy to photograph. I return to Boston two years later with Paul and Peter, where I start my second USA holiday and visit all the main attractions of the city. In some ways, its attraction is the link to the old country, but it's better known for the *Boston Tea Party* which started the process of the

Above: the Old State House *Right*: the New State House (author)

North

American States breaking away from England, finally sealed in 1776 with establishment of the United States of America. The original State House dates back to that time whilst the iconic Boston Common predates it by a wide margin. Boston is a very walkable city, and we enjoy its spacious city centre and particularly the Common where one gets views of old and new side by side.

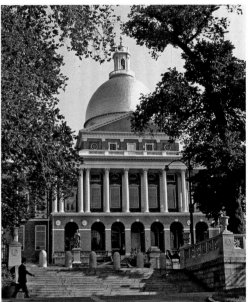

A PCC tram in Boston (author)

Cambridge, Massachusetts is three miles distant across the river from Boston and the journey affords the rider fine views back to the city and attractive Cambridge which presumably has links to its namesake in England. It is home to the world-famous Harvard University, whose campus covers a large area; the buildings in the city centre are of an early American red brick style which I find most attractive and which I find subsequently in Lancaster, Pennsylvania. The trip out to Cambridge is in a venerable old PCC Tram, of which there are many left in this city, a legacy of the lack of investment.

Above: The Sears Tower, towering above Union Station is, in 1980, the World's tallest building. In subsequent years, this title is overtaken in several Far East cities (author)

Chicago has to be for me, the greatest surprise of them all. Prior to my first trip, I knew little about it except for its notorious *Al Capone* past and when first transiting in 1978, am reluctant to step outside Union Station. Two years later, I get to know it better and find an elegant city centre of old and new skyscrapers, a lively feel, and the largest railroad centre in the USA. It's a buzzing commercial metropolis with better public transport than most and trains to all parts of the States; what's not to like!

When I step off the train from New Orleans in 1980, leave Union Station and see the city for the first time, I wonder why I have been so sceptical. The scene is lively and inviting, the city centre buildings are great (there was an architectural competition for radical new design in the 1960's) and there is an elevated metro railway in full view. I am with Paul and Peter and we stay in the *Ramada Inn* a few blocks from the station and have a full 25 hours to look around before we're off to Seattle the next afternoon. In 1981, we have only a few hours in transit between Detroit and St Louis so don't venture out of Union Station. We are able to look over the station's grand concourse (the only part of any architectural significance in an otherwise bland station).

It is in 1982 when we stay two nights in the city that we are able to appreciate more fully what a great place this is. The central business district (known as *The Loop* which is encircled by the *'El'* elevated metro) is where the most iconic buildings arising out of the architectural competition are found, including the Wrigley Building, headquarters of the chewing gum company.

Chicago is first and foremost a business city; hence its proliferation of high-rise office buildings, the then highest in the world is the Sears Tower. Ascending this building we are rewarded with a fantastic view over the city exemplifying, amongst other things, its vast railroad estate. We look down on a State penitentiary built in the shape of a triangle and see prisoners exercising on the roof. The whole Loop is clearly visible with its proliferation of tall buildings and we see Lake Michigan, which has a cooling influence and the reason it is called the Windy City.

The Wrigley building (centre), one of those iconic buildings dominating The Loop (author)

We explore The Loop, ride around on the 'El' and look for the remaining stations, *La Salle* (used by Rock Island trains) and site of closed *Dearborn* (the former Sante Fe terminus). The Board of Trade building forms a backdrop to both stations. We take a walk along the Lake Michigan foreshore where amongst other fine buildings is the original *Conrad Hilton Hotel*, forerunner of what is to become a worldwide empire and still very much to the fore today. The lakeside road is distinctly cooler, a refreshing change from the intense heat and noise experienced downtown. From Randolph Street station, we take an Interurban train to South Chicago. The CSS&SB* is the last of the interurban railways which were once commonplace in the USA, providing links between adjacent cities and outer suburbs. It is on life support and its rolling stock is old, dirty, and doesn't look like it can last long. However, some years' later, agreement is reached for new rolling stock which arrives none too soon. From initial scepticism, I've come full circle to love this city.

Left: on the second day, I take the opportunity to photograph the busy railroad scene south of Union Station, close to Amtrak's carriage servicing depot. Most trains from the station pass this way including the Burlington commuter trains. Here, a Burlington train to Aurora and an Amtrak train to Detroit leave together on parallel tracks (author)

* Chicago, South Shore & South Bend Railroad

Old San Francisco was, I believe, largely built by Chinese labourers and has retained a major Chinese presence ever since. It is now a thoroughly modern city close to Silicon Valley and makes alternative lifestyles its unique speciality. It is beautiful and very vibrant attracting huge numbers of visitors. I visit three times, in 1978, 1991 and finally in 1998 with Josiane for whom it is a dream come true! On my first visit, Paul and I stay with his friend Dick and wife in Daly City, south of the centre and terminus of the BART rapid transit. In true American fashion, the then new concept of rapid transit cannot be left to railroad engineers, reputedly stuck in an early 20th Century mind set so Boeing's aircraft engineers design it with the rail gauge 4'8" compared with international 4'8½" and a completely untried form of signalling; it is a disaster and a year on they are still trying to fit a square into a circle. San Francisco is defined for me by three icons; Fishermen's Wharf, Cable Cars and China Town and in 1978, Dick shows us round all three.

Above: there is a strong Chinese influence in the city (author)

Right: this is more like 'space age' San Francisco (author)

The cable car links downtown via Chinatown to Fishermen's Wharf and my first journey is a revelation. A strong brakesman is required to control the car through the rack rail beneath - requiring brute force at times - whilst also controlling revenue. In the afternoon, we travel to Oakland on the BART rapid transit and it appears the signalling system is not functioning well as there is a long section in the tunnel under the Bay limiting frequency to every ten minutes. We enjoy our ride to emerge in Oakland and continue to the terminus at Hayward.

In 1998 on Josiane's first visit to the USA, we arrive after crossing the Bay Bridge from Oakland as night is falling and she is enchanted by the tall buildings lit up along the shore. On our first day in the city, I'm keen that she visits the main attractions in the centre, travels on the iconic cable cars, sees Chinatown and visits Fishermen's Wharf, so that's what we do!

On the second day, we take a boat cruise from Fishermen's Wharf, circling the notorious island of Alcatraz and ending at Sausalito having passed under the famous Golden Gate Bridge. We are fascinated to see how a small island is almost completely taken over by the impregnable prison fortress from which very few escaped.

The approach to the Golden Gate Bridge is breathtaking and we see at least one reason for its name; a shiny bronze colour. Sausalito is a lively town on the Marin Peninsula, back on the mainland. Like the city, it appears to revel in an alternative lifestyle, and we enjoy looking round its chic shops before returning to San Francisco by bus, crossing the bridge, gaining another perspective of this amazing structure.

The famous and impressive Golden Gate Bridge (author)

On the third day, we visit Yosemite National Park (chap. 13). Day four is July the fourth, American Independence Day. After a day enjoying the city, we decide to take the cable car to Fishermen's Wharf for the celebrations which include a massive fireworks' display. There is a big queue for the cable car, but none comes; they are caught in congestion! Then something interesting happens; limousines appear offering $5 rides to the wharf. By the time one gets to us, the driver offers a $4 fare. The limo gets to the top of the hill and faces an almighty traffic jam on the other side, but we now have a grandstand view of the fireworks. At evening's end, we need to get back and see a cable car stuck on the hill. When it pulls up, we pile on and do what is done here, lean out from the footboards. The brakesman tells us he will reverse down the hill to

gain traction, then go like hell up the hill at speed, shouting *'hold on tight, we're gonna have a party, repel all boarders'* as we leave others standing at the car stop. The party continues to the terminus and we feel the spirit of the fourth of July! We eat a late dinner in a restaurant in Chinatown. There are a lot of memories to take back from this incredible city.

Party time for cable car riders on the Fourth of July! (author)

The Cathedral Basilica of St Francis of Assisi in Santa Fe (author)

What an incredible place Sante Fe is, even down to its original name *La Villa Real de la Sante Fe de San Francisco de Asis.* My first visit is in 1993 with Peter and Paul and when I introduce Josiane to the west five years later, include the city in our itinerary. It is a wise decision as she is as enchanted as I with the capital of New Mexico and one of America's oldest and certainly most historic cities, dating back to Native American times and part of the Spanish conquest of Mexico. Prior to my first visit in 1993, Sante Fe was better known to me as the given name of the Aitcheson, Topeka & Santa Fe Railroad, one of the giants of American railroading which perversely never served its namesake city. Though a city of over 80,000 inhabitants, its centre is compact and easily walkable. In that area, almost all buildings are in Adobe style fashioned from clay which makes them cool inside, protection from the harsh heat of summer.

Left: in the centre of the city is the marketplace with a long building and covered pavement which is where we discover beautiful art and jewellery from the Native Americans and others laid out on the pavement. Santa Fe turns out to be one of the major art centres of south west USA and we visit a couple of fascinating galleries in the city (author)

We visit most of the attractions including the diminutive Mission, one of the buildings opened by the missionaries on their quest to bring Christianity to the region; and the Cathedral of St Francis of Assisi, a prominent centrepiece of this fascinating city.

Left: the attractive Santa Fe Mission, one of hundreds of such places dotted over the mid-west and west of the USA. These were set up by Roman Catholic missionaries from the Iberian peninsula (author)

On my first visit, I was curious to see what existed of the branch line from Lamy on the former AT&SF main line and discover a freight terminal south of the city run by the Santa Fe Southern Railroad with one of its colourful red and yellow diesel locomotives parked outside. The system is a small one, just 20 miles to and from the 'Santa Fe' main line at Lamy, New Mexico. In recent years, it is to gain a new lease of life, being restored for passenger service by the State of New Mexico, who are also responsible for a commuter operation, *Rail Runner* between Santa Fe, Lamy and Albuquerque.

The Santa Fe Southern in 1993 (author)

Rail Runner commuter train 25 years on (shutterstock)

Classic and Colonial Charleston, a gracious city with an interesting history (author)

The final city in my selection may come as something of a surprise. It is included because it is a last minute decision to stop off on a journey Peter and I make in 1988 on the *Silver Meteor* between New York and Tampa, Florida, for no other reason I wished to see the city in which Gershwin's rock opera *Porgy and Bess*, a favourite of mine, is set.

The *Silver Meteor* arrives in Charleston at the unholy time of 05.15 hrs; unholy did I say, as we are greeted by a black nonconformist minister who is there trying to save to the souls of train passengers. We pass a few words though we are unexpectedly to meet again the next morning. For now, enquiring as to accommodation we are directed to a motel up the road and check in early. We discover that this is in North Charleston, over ten miles from the city centre and when we ask the receptionist about public transport, he stares at us blankly until he says *'oh you mean taxis!'*, any other form of transport clearly an alien concept to him. So, at this early hour, we enquire about breakfast and are directed to a *Waffle House* nearby which does a decent meal at a moderate price. After breakfast, we ask our server how to get to the city: *'you turn right outside the restaurant then right again which takes you to the interstate and its ten miles to the city'*. When we say we don't have a car, *'what, oh yo por guys'*!

We decide to start walking on the road parallel to the *Interstate* and propose to call a taxi when we get tired; no need to have worried as, after five minutes, we chance upon a bus stop and the timetable tells us there is a half-hourly service between 07.00 and 23.00 hrs at a one-way flat fare of 50c. A bus comes along a few minutes later almost full (all black people); now we know why white residents know nothing of public transport!

It's a fine city with lots of classic colonial style buildings and much of the day is spent walking around and enjoying the atmosphere.

Charleston's attractive waterfront (author)

We take a small boat to visit Fort Sumter in the afternoon complete with a running commentary. The Fort is on an island and the site of two of the most critical battles in the American Civil War, Charleston being a key Confederate stronghold.

Chalmers Street aka *Catfish Row* (author)

I am interested in seeing the fictional street *Catfish Row*, from rock opera *Porgy and Bess* and enquire at the tourist office. They don't know where it is and claim to know nothing about the opera based on Charleston, but it is a story about oppressed black people so presumably is blanked from their minds. Further enquiries lead me to Chalmers Street (*Catfish Row* in the opera) which is unprepossessing but at least I satisfy my curiosity. We return to our hotel by bus after an evening meal in the city.

Next morning, it is necessary to have an early rise as we need to catch the same train as we arrived on the previous day with a 05.30 hrs departure and we arrive at the station in good time to discover the *Silver Meteor* is two hours late. Our minister friend is again out bright and early chatting to all and sundry and we engage in conversation to find him a really interesting personality on a one-man mission to bring the gospel to travellers, and we hear him talk to blacks and whites alike about all manner of things, not just religion; a real 'one-off'. We board our train and head to Tampa, Florida to pick up a rental car and tour the Everglades National Park.

16   Crossing America By Train

Inspiring transcontinental journeys

North America is almost unique in having transcontinental railway journeys within one country.

In neither the USA or Canada are there through trains from coast to coast though the US achieved this for some years in the early 90's when the *Sunset Limited* operated between Floridian and Californian coasts.

Railways were pivotal in allowing both countries to open up their western territories, though not without considerable problems; in both cases the main barrier was the Rocky Mountains though other topographical features, not to mention native peoples, were obstacles to progress. While I

The Rockies provide a scenic backdrop to trans-continental routes *(shutterstock)*

do not set out to travel on all the current trans-continentals, it just happens over a period of 22 years. On three routes I go the whole way on one journey: Montreal to Vancouver, Chicago to Seattle and New Orleans to New York; others I do in stages with a gradual build until entire routes are covered. Every journey is a huge adventure; *America at See Level* as Amtrak puts it in one of its advertising campaigns. What better way to experience outstanding landscapes and great cities on a modest budget?

I hope, in the ensuing narrative to convey that sense of adventure, describe the journeys referring *inter alia* to interesting things that happen, people I meet and places I see. The routes so described are:

The *Canadian*, Montreal-Vancouver and the *Ocean*, Montreal-Halifax

The *Empire Builder*, Chicago-Seattle and Portland

The *California Zephyr*, Chicago-Oakland

The *Southwest Chief*, Chicago-Los Angeles

The *Sunset Limited*, Orlando-Los Angeles

The *Broadway Limited*, Chicago-New York

The *Coast Starlight*, Los Angeles-Seattle

The *Crescent*, New Orleans-New York

Sit back, relax and enjoy the journeys!

12:05

The Canadian

Ottawa
North Bay
Sudbury
Thunder Bay
Winnipeg
Regina
Calgary
Banff
Lake Louise
Vancouver

This map is taken from a late 1980's VIA Rail guide by which time the Canadian and Super Continental were combined to a single train starting from Toronto rather than Montreal

My first ever transcontinental journey: the westbound *Canadian* at Banff, Alberta in May 1978 (author)

The Canadian Pacific Railroad conjures up images of trains in amazing Rocky Mountain scenery and of contented passengers sipping their cocktails in a vista dome lounge. The reality on 23 May 1978 is a little different as Paul and I prepare to join the westbound *Canadian* for a three night/four day journey to Vancouver.

Montreal's Windsor station is down at heel and a tatty notice announces this great train. But it is still run by Canadian Pacific even though in a few months it will be a VIA Rail Canada train. Even in its faded glory, it is the icon it always was. The *Canadian's* Montreal portion is formed of original Canadian Pacific Budd stainless steel cars dating from 1954, six including domes and a beaver tail rear lounge, hauled by two General Motors E8 diesel-electric locomotives. Our sleeping car, *Mont Tremblant* consists of upper and lower berths lengthways to the train, curtained off from the central passageway. The train also has a dining car.

The route travelled is via the capital Ottawa (the station is several miles from the city) to Sudbury, Ontario, where a Toronto portion is attached taking the train size to 11 cars. The outskirts of Sudbury resembles the surface of the moon, caused by nickel ore mining, some of which finds its way to *International Nickel* at Clydach in the Swansea Valley, not far from my home.

At North Bay we cross the Ontario Northland Railway where ex-Trans Europe Express equipped *Northlander* is waiting to connect for Cochrane further north and soon after we pass the amusingly named Lake Nipissing. At dinner we experience the North American railway system of ordering from the menu, being supplied with our own slip and a pencil to write down our choices which are presented to the steward. We discover the British reserve of not speaking to fellow passengers doesn't hold in North America though it doesn't always work out well when an 87 year old man boasts incessantly about his journey, all the way from St John, New Brunswick to Winnipeg. Strangely, our barman is not too friendly, despite a large tip from Paul near the start of our journey. Unfortunately, he works through to Vancouver though the restaurant car crews change over several times and all put down their markers early deciding when and who to call for meals.

The *Canadian*, crossing the vast Canadian Shield, passing a CPR freight train (author)

On day two, we are travelling through a region known as the Canadian Shield which takes all day; it is a rocky and remote area with few settlements and is relatively flat. We arrive in late afternoon at Thunder Bay on the north bank of Lake Superior's western flank and are fascinated by its name; apparently it is of Native American origin and a merger of former twin towns Port Arthur and Fort William. We catch sight of massive grain trains consisting of up to 150 bogie tankers marked *Government of Canada-Gouvernement de Canade* and we will see many more as we head west. In the lounge we chat with Chris, a disaffected ex-Brit from Gloucestershire now living in Canada and travelling from Sudbury to holiday in Banff. Chris had emigrated as he disliked socialist Britain but is now getting to dislike the way he thinks Canada too is heading toward socialism; however, he made his fortune as a dentist here!

We arrive at Winnipeg, capital of Manitoba and one of Canada's major railway centres. By this time it is dark and I am momentarily startled by a loud bell ringing on the leading locomotive of a massive CP Rail freight passing through the station and find that all locomotives have to ring their bell in station limits, a custom that has clearly survived modernisation. Our train spends an hour for refuelling and servicing.

By the following morning we are further west into Saskatchewan and call at fascinatingly named stations such as Moose Jaw, Swift Current, Maple Creek and Medicine Hat. At the latter, I am invited into the cab of our E8 locomotive to look over the controls and chat to the engineer; it is not extended to a cab ride but is an interesting experience.

The view from the cab of our train locomotive, an E8 diesel, at Medicine Hat (author)

Later that day, we enter Calgary and get our first sight of oil wells, donkey engines and a characterless jungle of skyscrapers; better still, the distant Rocky Mountains. By early evening we are in Banff, where a large number of tourists join, filling the lounge and creating a convivial atmosphere into the night. Later the train reaches the famous Kicking Horse Pass followed by Lake Louise, a major crew changeover point, with many freight trains present; the weather has closed in and mars our view of the Rockies.

It is dark after Lake Louise, and by first light the train is dropping down along the Fraser River Canyon and we see the Canadian National route on the other side of the river all the way to Vancouver, arriving in its waterfront CPR station by mid-morning, and we check in at the *St Regis Hotel*. The afternoon is spent sightseeing in the city but prior to this I take a side trip to the CNR station to see the *Super Continental*; a train that was run by CN has now been taken on by VIA Rail. My return is by trolleybus via Chinatown and I'm fazed in finding myself on a bus full of Chinese people. Despite the rain, Vancouver is a most agreeable and cosmopolitan city, and we soak up its atmosphere.

Peter and I are to have a trip on the now combined *Canadian* and *Super Continental* from Jasper to Toronto in 1988 but that's another story.

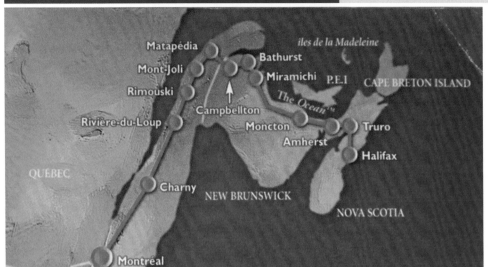

Left: route map of the *Ocean* at the turn of the century. A previous routing took it further south through northern Maine, USA (Via Rail publicity)

Below: The *Ocean* (*train on left of picture*) prepares to leave Montreal Central station. It is a long train needing two locomotives to provide train and 'hotel' power (author)

In 1978, I travelled three-quarters of the way across Canada and aim to make up for the other quarter 22 years later on the train to the coast in Nova Scotia. I am with Josiane (on her second visit to North America). She is bemused by this ambition of

mine to complete a coast-to-coast train trip across Canada but resigned to acceptance, which sees us on the *Ocean* overnight to Halifax, Nova Scotia. It leaves Montreal at 18.30 hrs and is to take 21 hours; the train is formed of classic Budd coaches dating from the early 1960's, extensively refurbished, including dining and sleeping cars. These coaches are to be replaced next year by British-built stock originally intended for Channel Tunnel overnight sleeper services.

We make the most of the classic rolling stock which is warm and comfortable. Shortly after leaving Montreal, dinner is served and we are seated opposite an old lady who is going to a funeral of a relative in Sydney, Nova Scotia, changing at Truro into a bus which will get her to destination five hours after we get to Halifax; however, she refuses to fly. All this is spoken in English, so I ask if she is English- or French- Canadian and confirms it is the latter, whereupon Josiane converses in French. When she leaves for her sleeper, I ask what they were talking about and Josiane has very little idea; the combination of an archaic form of French and thick accent makes for understanding difficulties!

Our sleeping accommodation is a twin-bed roomette with washroom and toilet, much like the original must have been, and beds are comfortable. I wake in the early hours to use the toilet, and when I flush, find with horror the handle won't return to normal and water keeps flowing; at this rate, it will surely drain our tank and possibly all the water in the coach. I summon the steward and to my surprise, he is there quickly. He checks and confirms that it's stuck open and *will* drain out all the water. He contacts a supervisor and arrangements are made for the coach to be topped up at Matapedia station at around 04.30 hrs. We are scheduled a 30-minute stop here which turns out to be an hour, the problem is solved, and a temporary fix made to our cabins' plumbing. Apparently, the age of the stock and fittings is proving an increasing problem and new ex- British Rail coaches can't come soon enough.

By daybreak, we are in New Brunswick and its fairly flat countryside which stays much the same as we cross into Nova Scotia after lunch. At Truro, we bid goodbye to the old lady and are thankful we don't have to put up with a five-hour onward bus journey. Something that has surprised me is how little freight traffic there is until I discover that another southerly route via northern Maine, direct and more easily graded, is the favoured freight routing. On arrival in Halifax Sunday afternoon, it is cloudy with a little rain and the city is pretty dead. Josiane expresses some displeasure at travelling all this time to such a place. We take a taxi to our well-appointed, comfortable hotel, suffer a power outage for some hours and eat by candlelight. Not our best day!

Looking across the river to the city of Halifax (author)

Aware that Josiane isn't exactly thrilled with Halifax, I rise early to look around the city in the hope that it is nicer than it looks. The signs are good, the sun is shining and it's quite warm as I venture to the historic quarter which I find very attractive with a strong maritime influence. It is a city of nearly half a million inhabitants with a large commercial shipping presence as the largest seaport on the east coast of the Americas. We spend the morning in the old city and later take a ferry across the river to Dartmouth, a small and most attractive town where we have lunch and look around.

Above: the historic town of Dartmouth, across the river from Halifax (author)

Below: the unusual (for me) sight of a 'commuter' plane at Halifax airport (author)

In the afternoon, we are persuaded to take a half day trip where it is anticipated we will see whales. When I tell our guide that we are going back to Wales tomorrow, he doesn't see the funny side; like most Americans, it's a country off their radar. In the event, it's a nice trip but we don't see any whales (out of season, apparently). We return to the hotel, book for dinner and I commit a *faux pas*. Our server is a young lady, similar in appearance to last night's server and when I say *'are you the young lady from Newfoundland',* get an icy response (a little local knowledge would have paid dividends here, I think!).

The following day is our last in North America and we take a taxi to the airport for our flight to Boston

connecting with the overnight journey back to London. Whilst awaiting departure, I am aware of a squadron of commuter planes taking people to remote parts of the mainland and islands off Nova Scotia, and Newfoundland. They are bussed from city to airport; an air commuter network, who would have believed it? Our flight arrives late from Boston, engine trouble apparently which is none too reassuring. They fix the problem and we leave

an hour late, our ancient turbo prop wheezing its way into the sky and along the coast down to Boston where we arrive nearly two hours late. Then it's back to Heathrow overnight and over Greenland.

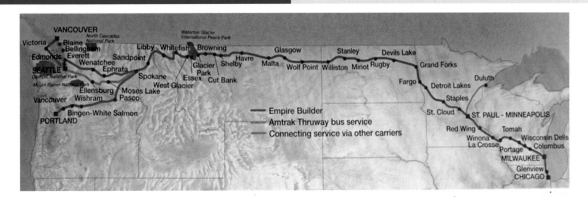

The *Empire Builder* has just left Cut Bank, Montana and we get our first view of the Rockies (author)

One of the USA's most iconic trains, named in honour of James J Hill, who opened up the north-west USA by amalgamating several railroads into the Great Northern. Inaugurated in 1929, I've travelled on it twice, in 1980 from Chicago to Seattle and in 1993 to Portland. My narrative describes the 1980 journey with brief references to 1993. My first introduction to the *Empire Builder* is in June 1980, accompanied by Paul and Peter; I am to make my longest train journey in the USA to date from Chicago to Seattle, a schedule of 45 hours over two nights. The train has recently delivered *Superliner* double deck coaches heralding a new and most enjoyable way of travelling and seeing the country. The pedestrian pace to Milwaukee makes me muse that the route once hosted the *Hiawathas*, the world's fastest trains.

It is to be thirteen years on in June 1993 when Peter and I use this train again, though this time it is to get to Portland, Oregon. We leave Chicago in the morning travelling to Milwaukee, an interesting city even if it no longer brews *Schlitz, the beer that made Milwaukee famous* and we are fortunate to chance upon a large and very colourful carnival in the city centre.

From Milwaukee the line veers north-west reaching and crossing the mighty Mississippi at La Crosse, Wisconsin with the ensuing run along the riverside in the low evening sunlight to St Paul, is a delightful trip. In 1993 the weather is not as good and the scenic journey along the Mississippi is marred by cloud; the river is running very high and we learn later that extreme flooding is experienced right along the river valley. A crisis always brings out wit and I am amused at a report of a large hoarding at a downriver Mississippi settlement: *coming soon to a city near you, the Mississippi*!

Left: the *Empire Builder* has a fuelling stop at Midway Station, St Paul-Minneapolis. This type of operation is commonplace on Amtrak trains enabling locomotives to run the entire journeys. It is here that I get a reality check on the special requirements for servicing trains on trans-continental journeys. Fuel is supplied under contract here from a company called 'Hassett' who, it seems 'has it' (author)

The metropolis of St Paul/Minneapolis is served by a station midway between the two and the train pauses here for a twenty-minute refuelling stop. It continues to Fargo, North Dakota reached after midnight; one wonders if there is any connection with the noted *Wells Fargo* stagecoach line. At daybreak, and still in North Dakota, Montana is reached a few hours later. The States' strapline *Big Sky Country* aptly describes Montana with endless views of rolling hills, grassland and pasture, pleasant, though it becomes monotonous. There are frequent grain elevators at trackside giving a clue to a principal activity in this State.

Any monotony ends on arrival at Cut Bank in mid-afternoon and our first sight of the Rocky Mountains, though the weather deteriorates as we go further, and night comes on. Before nightfall we notice vast areas of forest badly singed by fire and realise it has been caused by the massive Mount St Helens volcanic eruption two weeks earlier which devastates vast areas of inland Washington State. The railway and train seem unaffected though there is a thickness of ash at trackside; Spokane is reached just before midnight. From there, the train is routed through the Stampede Pass where more evidence of the eruption is noted with inches-deep volcanic dust everywhere, creating a surreal sight. Arriving at Seattle at breakfast, we see that the locomotive and coach bogies are caked in volcanic dust. Later, in the taxi, our driver tries to sell us test tubes of it as a souvenir which we politely decline!

Thirteen years later, from our sleeping berths, we are unaware of the shunting that goes on at Spokane where the Portland portion leaves about ten minutes behind the Seattle portion. We wake to see the high country around Pasco known as the Camas Prairie and at Wishram, the line runs along the north bank of the Columbia River through to Portland. On the other bank of the river is the Union Pacific route which we used on the *Pioneer* in 1980. At Portland, we pick up a car and explore the amazing Oregon coastal road, one of the most beautiful in the world, explained in greater detail (chap. 13).

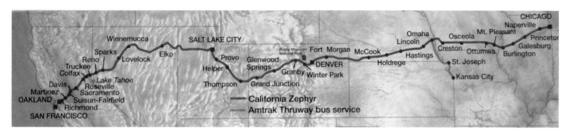

1998 motive power is *Genesis* P40 diesels on the *California Zephyr* at Emeryville, California (author)

This famous train had its 'genesis' in the 1940's when the Burlington, Rio Grande and Western Pacific Railroads combined to compete with the Union Pacific and Sante Fe for the lucrative California passenger traffic. It was one of a family of *Zephyrs* serving the principal cities of the west and mid-west and discontinued with the inauguration of Amtrak, reborn as the *San Francisco Zephyr* until the 1980's when it regains its original title. I make three journeys on this train, in 1978 from Denver to Oakland, in 1980 eastbound from Denver to Chicago and finally in 1998 from Oakland to Denver.

My first acquaintance with the train, known then as the *San Francisco Zephyr* is in 1978 at Denver Union Terminal. It is to be our home for the one and a half days' journey to Oakland, California, across the Bay from San Francisco. It's a long train formed of 1950/60's Budd stainless steel stock hauled by two General Motors' SDP40 locomotives; two are needed to lift the train over heavy grades through hilly southern Wyoming. An initial surprise is that it reverses out of Union Station for a mile before joining the Union Pacific main line. The route is through Wyoming, a state that nowadays has no Amtrak service and we remain in that state for the rest of daytime, crossing to Utah in the evening.

There is excitement as we see real cowboys close to lineside and drama ensues as a train enthusiast comes over on the public address with information on passing freight trains until cautioned by the conductor who apologises to those for whom it is of no interest!

Connection is made to the northbound *Pioneer* at Ogden after which our train crosses the Great Salt Lake followed by the Nevada Desert in the night, arriving at Sparks, a stop for fuel and crew changeover. Shortly after is the gambling city of Reno, second only to Las Vegas. Thereafter, the train starts a long haul over spectacular Donner Pass, one of the most difficult lines constructed in the west; after this it drops down to the state capital of California at Sacramento. From here it is a pleasant journey along the Carquinez Strait and outer suburbs of the Bay Area, terminating at Oakland (after a mile of running along the median strip of its main street). As there was never a railway bridge over San Francisco Bay, we take a rail link bus to reach the city at its Transbay Terminal.

My next appointment with the *Zephyr* is June 1980 when it is the final train trip of a three-week holiday. With Paul and Peter, I board the eastbound journey to Chicago late in the evening. Not yet equipped with *Superliners*, the *Budd* single-level coaches are in poor condition with dubious air conditioning, the train is full, creating a hot, sticky and crowded overnight trip which is our worst USA train journey so far.

The Donner Pass in the benign conditions of early summer (author)

Twenty years on from my first trip on the *Zephyr*, many things have changed. The train is formed of *Superliner* double deck coaches, now nearly twenty years old, the most modern Amtrak P42 *Genesis* locomotives and it has a new name, the *California Zephyr* and is routed along the former *Rio Grande* between Salt Lake City and Denver instead of the Wyoming route of 1978. In early July 1998, Josiane and I are to take it from Emeryville, California (the modern replacement for the Oakland terminal) to Grand Junction, Colorado, a 26-hour journey and it's her first experience of an overnight train. We are due to leave Emeryville at 09.45 hrs but all is not well; the previous days' arrival from Chicago was very late and the train is still catching up on overnight servicing. We leave an hour late, everything seems fine and as we eat lunch at Sacramento a further delay is announced; apparently, there is some difficulty with losing air in the brakes.

The problem is fixed but the train needs to stop twice more between here and Reno for the same reason. I think they should just replace the air pipe rather than tape it up to stop the leak. Despite this, we are pleased there is an on-board volunteer guide who regales us with the dramatic history of the early pioneers transiting the Donner Pass in winter and the awful problems they encountered including many deaths. This initiative is welcome as it puts our relatively comfortable journey in context. The train is almost three hours late arriving in Sparks, a suburb of Reno, where there is a crew changeover. Two new conductors join and tell us they have fifty years train running experience between them and reckon they can fix the problem. So they replace the defective air pipe, no problem! Due to the late running, it is dark when we reach the Nevada desert though peering out of the window, all we see is a ghostly picture as much of the desert is formed of salt deposits which glow white in the darkness.

We settle into our en-suite sleeping accommodation with upper and lower berths and Josiane is impressed by how much is squeezed into a small space without looking crowded; and even more so with a coffee machine outside which we can use at any time. It is over three hours behind schedule at Salt Lake City and as it is daylight, we are able to enjoy the stunning scenery as we travel through Utah. Arrival at Grand Junction, Colorado is in late afternoon and I arrange a car here for a weeks' touring of Colorado and New Mexico.

No doubt about who owns this station! Salt Lake City (author)

A week later, we are back in Grand Junction and find a hotel in the town close to the train station. Whilst Josiane is enjoying a bath, I venture out to find a place to eat and there is a *Denny's* right opposite. Back at the hotel, I switch on TV and get the news on a local channel; the main item is about a motorcyclist involved in a drive by shooting *last night outside Denny's in Grand Junction!* As lightning doesn't usually strike twice in the same place, I say nothing to Josiane until we return from our meal.

The following day we re-join the eastbound *California Zephyr* at Grand Junction after a leisurely breakfast. It is on time and the trip east which I have done before is one of the most scenic train journeys anywhere in the world and we greatly enjoy travelling through deep canyons of the Colorado River and wild mountain scenery. After passing through the famous Moffat Tunnel the conductor announces over-running track maintenance ahead and we wait well over an hour for this to clear; at least we have a great view. As the train approaches Denver Union station, it is held for a long Burlington Northern freight train to cross on the level and it takes over half an hour to do so, with a two-hour late arrival.

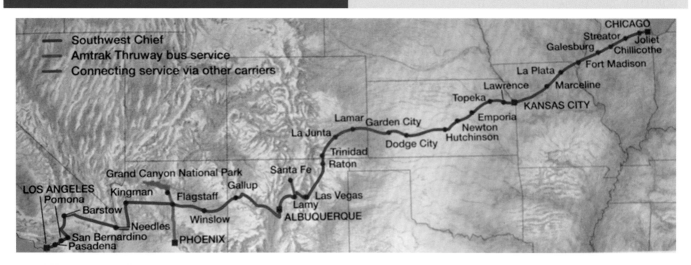

The predecessors to this train, the *Chief* and *Super Chief*, were arguably among the most glamorous transcontinental trains of their period. They were the brainchild of go-ahead Aitcheson, Topeka and Santa Fe railroad in intense competition for the lucrative California passenger trade before the days of the jet airline. So iconic were these that at the inception of Amtrak in 1971, the Santa Fe refused permission for either name

Above: iconic Santa Fe passenger locomotive livery

Right: Los Angeles Union Passenger Terminal, one of America's most attractive train stations (both photos by the author)

to be used on the successor service; its initial name was the anodyne *Southwest Limited* and only after introduction of *Superliner* coaches did it approve the quality uplift.

I make three journeys, in 1978 eastbound then 1981 westbound and finally 1993 eastbound, the latter two journeys over only part of the route.

In early June 1978, Paul and I have just spent a day in Los Angeles having visited Universal Studios in Hollywood and the city's Mexican market. That night we board the *Southwest Limited* for Flagstaff, Arizona. The train is one of only three long-distance trains to leave Los Angeles Union Passenger Terminal this day, such is the reduction in long distance train travel in the USA.

At dinner, our companion is an LA businessman going to Arizona, a regular monthly trip for him, doing business with the Indians; Paul reckons he is going to collect the rent! He is of the opinion that we were unwise to go to the Mexican market where he believes white people are considered unwelcome! Arrival at Flagstaff is around 07.30 hrs where take a bus link to the Grand Canyon; we first seek accommodation which is an antique shop with rooms in the main street, drop our bags and off to the bus depot for the two-hour journey run by *Nava-Hopi Tours* to the south rim of the Canyon. It truly blows our minds, and we spend most of the day there, though don't venture into the canyon. We return early evening; at the hotel the owner sleeps on the floor of his antique shop and agrees to call us early.

The *Southwest Limited* arriving at Flagstaff, Arizona on a warm, sunny morning (author)

No morning call comes though we wake in time and on the way, trip over the manager in his sleeping bag! We settle the bill and leave to take the train on to Chicago. It is formed of ex Santa Fe *Hi-Level* coaches, forerunner of Amtrak's *Superliners*, still a poor relation of the *Super Chief*. The journey is through semi-desert and scrubland with occasional settlements and stations through Arizona and New Mexico. We are amused by our barman with his southern *lilt* coming through the train trying to sell his ice-cold milk. *'Hey folks, ya must buy ma ars col' milk to getcha over the Rockies'*. He finally gets a buyer *'Misser, you's goin' to make it over the Rockies - don' no about them other folks'*.

At Albuquerque, the train stops for servicing, including a side wash with a machine sporting a brush reaching the top of the hi-level cars. From here the train takes the secondary route over the famous Raton Pass, and we note a lot fewer freight trains. We are close to the state capital Santa Fe on reaching Lamy; it's curious that a great railroad as this never served its namesake city!

Travelling overnight we reach Kansas City at around 05.30 hrs; in an adjacent platform is the *National Limited* departing an hour later for its day and a half journey to New York via Indianapolis and fated for withdrawal in 1979 never to return. It's a long journey through flat and uninteresting country until we get into the limits of the Chicago metropolitan area. At Joliet, we cross the Chicago, Rock Island & Pacific route used by the *Quad Cities Rocket* and Rock Island commuter trains from La Salle Street. I spot a massive marshalling yard and TOFC*/container terminal at Cicero outside Chicago and arrive at Union station which has recently replaced the former Dearborn AT&SF station. *Trailer on Flat Car, trucks on rail wagons

By the time of my next trip in 1981, the train is formed of *Superliner* coaches but is still awaiting approval for a name upgrade. It is to be a relatively short journey by American standards, the 503 miles from Kansas City, Missouri to Lamar, Colorado. Paul, Peter and I are en route from St Louis to Denver. The train is full and I am assigned a seat next to a young lady who researches the *Sante Fe* and *Oregon pioneers t*rails. We arrive in legendary Dodge City at dawn to witness torrential rain and cattle stockyards stretching as far as the eye can see and a surreal sight of thousands of cattle up to their knees in oozing mud!

My third and final trip on this train in 1993, again with Paul and Peter, is from Albuquerque, New Mexico to Chicago. We have had a wonderful few days' in southern Colorado and northern New Mexico. We have pre-arranged to turn our rental car in at Albuquerque, from where we are to take the train at 14.15 hrs to Chicago. We arrive in the city about an hour before and head for the train station. Albuquerque doesn't appear to offer much of interest except that we see a street marked *Route 66* so that's another famous landmark to tick off our list. At the station, the agent tells us the train, now the *Southwest Chief* is on time so we stay in the waiting room. Then it gets dramatic as we spot an approaching tornado and seek shelter in the lee of the wind. Peter has the presence of mind to take a photo of the skyscraper opposite in sunlight and then two minutes later, enveloped in swirling black dust! It's a scary scene which we watch from our protected position. A downside, the station agent tells us that the train has been delayed by two-hours due to a signalling outage.

It eventually leaves around 16.00 hrs and proceeds slowly for the next couple of hours due to the grade and signalling problems. The famous Raton Pass, which, because of steep grades limiting train loads, has been reduced to a secondary route as freight uses a level route further south. We traverse Colorado and most of Kansas in darkness and arrive in Kansas City three hours late. A further delay is announced due to a defect on the dining car so we are there for over an hour. Every cloud has a silver lining and mine is watching freight on the adjacent four tracks, one after another, for the whole hour. I count the total number of wagons that passed (c.1200) and quickly calculate if they were trucks, not trains, there would be one truck per second passing, amazing and what an advertisement for rail freight! The journey on to Chicago is uneventful and we make up little time, arriving there at 19.00 hrs.

Above: a flashback to our 1981 trip when we spot a Sante Fe business train in Kansas City station. It is hauled by three AT&SF ex-*Super Chief* passenger diesels now on freight duties. The coaches are from the *Chief's* super fleet (author)

176

The Sunset Limited

Los Angeles to New Orleans & Miami

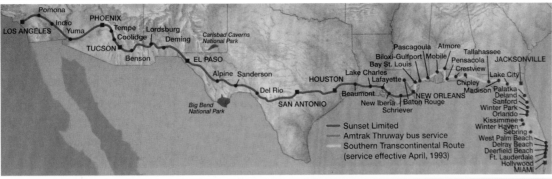

A pair of General Motors PC30 locomotives on the *Sunset Limited* at Phoenix Arizona in 1981 (author)

The *Sunset Limited* dates back to Southern Pacific days and a surprise addition to the Amtrak network in 1971, since when it has been a tri-weekly operation. I make two journeys on the train, first in 1981 between Los Angeles and San Antonio, and twelve years later - by then promoted to become the only true transcontinental train in America - between Orlando, Florida and El Paso, Texas.

My first journey is in early June 1991 with Paul and Peter. We have been to San Diego and enjoy a superb run along the Californian coast that afternoon before picking up the *Sunset Limited* leaving at 22.30 hrs for the 2032 miles journey to New Orleans. We are taking this as far as Phoenix for another visit to the Grand Canyon. Most of the journey is in darkness, with arrival in Phoenix at 06.30 hrs which, even at that hour, is very warm. We take a rental car for several days to the Grand Canyon and back.

We take up the same train, which as on the previous trip, is hauled by a two P30 locomotives, a newer design than the F40 and found mainly on the *Sunset* and *Texas Eagle* routes. It is the start of a marathon journey of three days almost continuous travelling to New York.

We have already made sleeping reservations for the third nights' travel on the *Broadway* from Chicago (one sleeper, two *slumbercoach* berths) but faced with a prospect of the first two nights on reclining seats, we seek berths on the *Sunset*. The conductor has none available so we are resigned to a first night on recliners.

Leaving Phoenix at 06.45 hrs (Arizona local time is an hour later than Mountain Time) so a 05.15 hrs Central Time arrival at San Antonio is more like 02.15 hrs! The train goes through desert for mile after mile with two stops in Arizona and two in New Mexico, arriving El Paso, Texas late afternoon. Near Deming, New Mexico, I look across a vast expanse of desert and see a large lake on the horizon, but on getting closer - it's not there - it's a mirage so I understand the frustration of the earlier pioneers when desperately seeking water!

Desert scene near Deming, New Mexico seen from the train (author)

El Paso station looks like an industrial estate fallen on hard times, bearing little resemblance to one serving a city of 600,000 people. After a servicing stop we are off, now firmly in Texas for the 600 miles run to San Antonio, much of it overnight in reclining seats. Arrival in San Antonio is at 05.30 hrs which due to time zone change feels much earlier; we are shattered and have a three hour wait for our connection. I can't sleep so walk into the city in search of the *Alamo*; by the time I find it, I need to dash back to get the bus to San Antonio's Missouri Pacific station for the *Inter American* to Chicago; it's alongside a marshalling yard, just a sign stuck in the gravel and no shelter; unbelievable!

It is June 1993 when I join the *Sunset Limited* at Orlando, recently extended from New Orleans to Miami now the longest route in the USA at 3,066 miles. Everyone who travels to Orlando goes there for its major attractions, but we are simply in transit to get overland to New Mexico and have all day before taking the train which leaves around 18.30 hrs. With *Mickey Mouse* not in our plans, we head for the city and find it is at least a century old with an attractive historic core that's worth exploring. The station is several blocks away and we go there in early evening and see local freight trains, operated by Florida Central Railroad.

The tri-weekly *Sunset Limited* arrives; it heads north to Jacksonville passing through the Florida Panhandle during the night. We miss sight of State Capital, Tallahassee, where it calls around 03.00 hrs; daylight comes and it is still in Florida, over an hour late. At Atmore, Alabama, I spot an Amtrak train that isn't in the time-table; it's a special between Mobile and Montgomery put on to relieve local interstate congestion. Next is Mobile, for some reason a place that has always held a fascination for me; in reality, it looks unexciting.

Not so, the *Big Bayou Canot* on the Mobile River a little further on which is to earn notoriety three months later when the bridge is struck by a barge as the eastbound *Sunset* is crossing, resulting in three locomotives and several coaches plunging into the bayou in the early morning, killing 47 and injuring 103*. Our train proceeds through the industrialised Mississippi coast to reach New Orleans almost two hours late. It has a scheduled layover of two hours now reduced to 20 minutes so there is no opportunity to take a quick look at the city.

Left: the remarkable Huey P Long Bridge over the Mississippi at New Orleans (*wikipedia public domain*)

Below: the *Sunset Limited* on arrival at El Paso, Texas. The locomotive is a non-standard type and livery (author)

We are to be on this train for another 24 hours and arrange an upgrade to sleeping accommodation for when we leave Houston, scheduled at 22.30 hrs. On resuming, there follows the most amazing manoeuvre I've had on a train as it crosses the Mississippi on a high bridge, a long gradual ascent, including a spiral to gain sufficient height and the same in reverse the other side; and experience breath-taking views from high above the river! On this part of the journey, I am hoping to see the famous bayou country that characterises the Gulf Coast and am bitterly disappointed with the obscene amount of development and drainage that has taken place. The journey continues in similar vein to Houston Texas, reached after passing massive oil and chemical complexes, big oil country!

We take to our sleepers from here and sleep soundly, waking at Del Rio, 180 miles west of San Antonio; the

sleeper upgrade includes restaurant meals, so we head to the diner for breakfast which helps relieve the boredom; southern Texas just goes on and on. We finally make El Paso around 14.00 hrs, and we are to pick up a car here. We take a taxi to a car rental office and notice the city is in better shape than its train station. We drive north and soon cross the border into New Mexico, next day to explore northern New Mexico and Colorado.

*a railway engineer colleague told me he had been invited to attend the public enquiry into this accident as an expert witness. He relates that he responded to an old lady questioning whether people fallen in the river were at risk of being eaten by alligators, *'Madam, if you were an alligator swimming up the river in the dark and hundreds of tons of bridge and train come tumbling down, wouldn't you be swimming furiously back to the Gulf of Mexico in no time!*

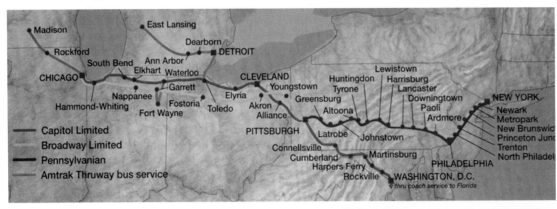

The *Broadway Limited* waits a *long time* at Monroeville, Pennsylvania (find out why below)

My association with one of the giants of the Pennsylvania Railroad, the *Broadway Limited* is not to go smoothly, to put it mildly. The train, featured in many Hollywood films but memorably in *The Sting*, survives into Amtrak, which is eliminating silver service in the dining car the day after we travel.

On this occasion in early June 1981, the *Broadway Limited* is the last of three trains on our very long and eventful journey from Phoenix to New York and, after two successive nights' fitful sleep on reclining seats, I'm looking forward to a pre-reserved luxurious roomette; the silver service dining will be a bonus too! My friends and I arrive in Chicago and have over five hours before our final overnight journey on the *Broadway*, former flagship of the Pennsylvania Railroad. It is to be the last time for silver service dining on this train so ensure we book dinner. Our sleeper reservations include a luxurious roomette and two slumber coach berths (couchettes) so I bag the roomette to get a proper nights' sleep. The train leaves at 19.30 hrs, we are served a really fine dinner and turn in early to our sleeping accommodation, little realising the drama which is to unfold. I pass a peaceful night and am briefly aware of calling at Pittsburgh around 06.30 hrs after which it all happens! An hour later, the train stops for an extended period during which time I am propositioned by two ladies of the night. Even if I wanted their services, which I don't, I'm still pretty tired and despatch them in short order.

Shortly after, the train (all 16 coaches) reverses at speed and I consult my *Rand McNally* atlas to see on what alternative route we could be diverted. But no, we stop at the one-horse Pennsylvania town of Monroeville that is to become our home for the next eight hours! A few minutes later I hear sirens and police, fire and ambulance services arrive; firemen leap aboard asking if people feel unwell and if so, will be taken to hospital in one of the school buses which have just appeared on the scene; my only feeling is of hunger as it's well past nine. I ask one of the firemen what the problem is and he reluctantly says: *'they think that chemicals from a leaking rail tank car may have gotten into the air conditioning!'* Those that don't go to hospital are asked to detrain and await developments; we need to be very patient!

It's a warm sunny day and we, like many others, go to a coffee shop, which is overwhelmed. At the scene, chaos reigns as emergency services vie for superiority. CBS News arrives by helicopter and interviews a lady next to me, putting words in her mouth: *'wouldn't you say ma'am that this is all the fault of Conrail'* and she agrees (and is probably right!). There is no sign of anyone from Conrail or Amtrak taking charge or even being there. In late afternoon word comes that the 'all clear' has been given for the train to proceed and it

leaves around 16.30 hrs. The chemical theory is confirmed true, but it's identified as harmless type used in the making of perfumes; it seems that US rail tankers don't display *Hazchem* codes on vehicles or if they do, nobody understands them! The trains' catering crew steps up and prepares a massive pile of sandwiches given free to all passengers. The journey proceeds uneventfully over the famous Horseshoe Curve, the iconic bridge over the Susquehanna River at State capital, Harrisburg, and on to Lancaster where we alight at 20.30 hrs and check into a hotel.

Left: Horseshoe Curve, Altoona (*Jim Olmstead, the Conrail Historical Society collection*)

After a night's sleep and relaxing morning, we take the *Keystone Service*, changing at Philadelphia to the *Yankee Clipper* to New York. My friends both do some shopping before heading to the airport; I remain in Penn station and look in on the Amtrak tours office. I talk with a young lady who books people on to inclusive tours by train. Enquiring as to whether themed tours were done, she is intrigued, asking what I have in mind. *'What about a disaster movie set on a train; like a train's air conditioning becomes infected with poisonous chemical fumes from a leaking freight tank car',* I suggest. She is surprised though reasons that such movies exaggerate for effect and thought it would be impractical to stage. So I tell her it really happened yesterday on the eastbound *Broadway* and she shrieks; she knows nothing of this and I suspect nobody else in Amtrak does either! I rendezvous with my friends and we're off to JFK airport for our flight home.

This journey was at one time advertised by the Southern Pacific Railroad as the most beautiful train journey in the world and after three journeys over the Californian coast section, I can well believe it. Back in the SP days, there were several *Daylight* services between Los Angeles and the Bay Area (San Francisco and Oakland) and the *Starlight* service which ran day and night through to Seattle. The latter survives to the present day and explains the unusual nomenclature.

Left: the route of the *Coast Starlight* *Above*: the *Coast Starlight* on the Pacific Coast between Santa Barbara and San Luis Obispo where the railway traverses virgin coastline for over 50 miles. (Amtrak)

It is in June 1978 that I make my first journey on this route accompanied by Paul. We have been staying with Paul's friends in Daly City, San Francisco and Dick takes us in the morning to South San Francisco for a Southern Pacific commuter train to San Jose, where we are to change and await the arrival of the *Coast Starlight*. . The Peninsula Line is the sole remaining commuter route in California and still privately operated by Southern Pacific and it is our first experience of double deck coaches in the USA. The *Coast Starlight* consist is all single level Budd stainless steel coaches dating from the 1950/60's with a sprinkling of dome cars and we are treated to a scenically delightful journey, much of it along the Pacific coast. It is inland to San Luis Obispo, where we wait a short time for the northbound train to pass.

Shortly after leaving San Luis Obispo the train reaches the coast and travels for the next 50 miles above virgin beach and coastline not accessible by any other transport (this is because landward of the railway is a massive air force base with restricted entry).

The next major call is the fine city of Santa Barbara after which we move inland again and are soon aware of the Los Angeles megalopolis, exemplified by a distant brown haze of polluted air. Arrival at LA is in early evening and we head by taxi to pre booked accommodation at a *Travelodge* in downtown. It is in a pretty unsavoury part of the city and the front desk man sits protected by iron bars. On enquiring about a meal, he directs us to the only restaurant close by; it is Japanese. In darkness, we sprint 200 yards to the restaurant

Left: A busy scene at San Luis Obispo in summer 1978 as passengers join and alight. The northbound train crosses here and crews changeover. The journey south of here is one of the finest in the world! (author)

taking our luck on the meal and its fine! The next day we visit Hollywood and other parts of LA before proceeding east to Arizona and the Grand Canyon.

My second journey on the *Coast Starlight* in 1991 is to be the longest of three and the only one in which it travels under starlit skies. I am accompanied by Peter and the holiday starts with a visit to the Sacramento Rail Fair followed by a tour of California east of the Rockies. Following a train journey from Sacramento to Bakersfield and bus connection to Santa Barbara, we join the train there on a fine day in mid-May. We are to leave at noon for the longest train journey of this holiday on the *Starlight* through to Seattle; it has a dismal on time record and is an hour late leaving. Since my initial journey in 1978, the train has been equipped with double deck *Superliners* which include a panoramic lounge with seaward-facing seats; and there is 50 miles of virgin Pacific coastline between here and San Luis Obispo.

At San Luis Obispo, we cross the southbound train which has been waiting for us, having arrived on time. Hereon, we head through mountainous country, past a large bird and nature reserve, before dropping down to San Jose and through the megalopolis that is the east of San Francisco Bay. Oakland is reached at 21.30 hrs and as we see San Francisco light up across the Bay, our train is beginning to live up to its name. It heads through mountainous northern California in darkness and it is not until it gets into Oregon that daylight comes, and we have missed seeing the iconic Mount Shasta. Klamath Falls is reached at breakfast time and we take in the view of its large lake before heading into the Cascade Mountains, Eugene and state capital Salem, reaching Portland in early afternoon. The journey north from Portland is more familiar territory for us and we are all entertained by our conductor who runs a trivial pursuit game from his cabin. Arrival at Seattle is in late evening and we check into the *Vance Hotel*. It is raining hard and tomorrow, we are to take the *Alaska Marine Highway* (Chap. 11), so we check the weather forecast, which is unremittingly bad!

My final journey on the *Coast Starlight* is in June 1998 with Josiane who is thrilled with California (first time here) and cannot believe how beautiful a train journey can be.

Above: this is how the Southern Pacific *Daylight* and *Starlight* trains looked in their glory days with the livery style continued through locomotive and train. The train is recreated in 1991 and seen at Carquinez between Oakland and Sacramento (author)

We start our holiday in San Diego and travel along the Pacific coast on a *Pacific Surfliner* and alight at Santa Barbara, arriving five hours later and stay at the fabulous *Pepper Tree Inn*; so good in fact that even with the prospect of our scenic train trip, we have to drag ourselves out of the hotel next day.

Left: a *Superliner* sightseer lounge is probably one of the finest features of the present day with fifty miles of virgin Pacific coast to view between Santa Barbara and San Luis Obispo (Amtrak)

The *Starlight* duly rolls in around 13.00 hrs and we board in great anticipation of the journey to come. I have previously experienced the route and am prepared for the scenic ride above the Pacific coast though Josiane isn't and she is completely bowled over, not just by the view but the double-deck sightseer lounge with outward facing seats. At San Luis Obispo, we pass the southbound train and then climb steeply on a switchback route with a backdrop of more wind turbines than I have seen anywhere else. The route follows the Salinas River valley, a wildfowl park and San Jose, centre of Silicon Valley. From here to Oakland is completely built up and as the train is running late, it's dark by the time we reach Emeryville, the main station in Oakland. We connect into an Amtrak bus to cross the Bay to San Francisco and get the most wonderful view of the city's skyscrapers lit up; it's magic! A great prelude to a great city and we spend a most enjoyable week in San Francisco, visit all the attractions and include a trip to Yosemite National Park.

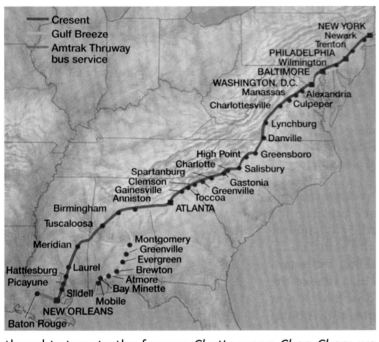

The Crescent, previously known as the *Southern Crescent*, was a flagship of the innovative Southern Railway. Its name derives from New Orleans, known as the *Crescent City*. When Amtrak is formed in 1971, Southern is one of three companies that opt to continue service in their own name to maintain quality. In 1979, Southern finally cedes to Amtrak.

My first journey on the *Crescent* is in June 1980 when I travel with Peter and Paul from Washington to New Orleans. Until recently, this train, then the *Southern Crescent* was hauled by a pair of Southern Railway E type diesels in attractive green and white livery. On the train, thoughts turn to the famous *Chattanooga Choo Choo*; we have dinner in the diner (though in Virginia not Carolina as we are running late) and I have my first introduction to pecan pie. By the time we are eating our

ham and eggs we are well past Carolina and almost into Atlanta, Georgia. The trip through Georgia and Alabama is heavily forested country, generally flat though not featureless. Arriving in New Orleans, there is a painfully slow terminal arrival through a one-mile backup move, reversing the whole train into the station.

Above: the *Crescent* at New Orleans in 1980. Amazingly, this long train reverses out of the station for more than a mile to gain the main line to the north (author)

My next trip on the 'Crescent' is in September 2000 on my second visit to America with Josiane. We have started our holiday in New Orleans, a fine city with a strong French connection which is great for Josiane who is French. We have had a good few days including cheering on presidential hopeful Al Gore (who lost to George W Bush), and a paddle steamer trip on the Mississippi.

Paddle steamer *Natchez* on the Mississippi at New Orleans (author)

On the morning of 9 September, we have an early start to the longest journey on a single train that Josiane has ever taken; 1378 miles from New Orleans *Big Easy* to New York *Big Apple* scheduled to take 31 hours. *The Crescent* is formed of relatively new *Viewliner* rolling stock; higher than a standard single-level coach to allow lower and upper level sleeping berths. In line with USA practice these are arranged longitudinally rather than transverse as in the UK and Europe. We have reserved a roomette throughout which converts from sleeper to day compartment and vice versa. Each coach is assigned a customer service host and ours is a pleasant young lady from New Orleans who does this route regularly and recommends it as a friendly one.

First landmark is the thirty-mile trestle over Lake Pontchartrain where it's difficult to see the north shore; it's like a journey across the sea! Shortly after, we are in Mississippi and remain in that State for some hours. Its landscape is a mixture of bayou and forest and as we move on to Alabama it becomes much more forested. We notice frequent settlements here and in Georgia have a lot of churches and we start a contest to see who can spot the most. This is the *Bible belt*, broken only by the ugly industrial landscape around Birmingham, Alabama's largest city. Atlanta, Georgia is reached in the evening, and the train stops for forty minutes for servicing. It's a pleasant evening and we alight and view the distant downtown skyscrapers. Our ticket package includes all meals, so we head to the diner after leaving Atlanta. By the time we enter South Carolina, it is dark. We pass through the Carolinas and much of Virginia in darkness and when we wake, are in Manassas, Virginia, only thirty miles from Washington DC; the journey north is through commuter-land as many of those working in Washington live in this state.

The Capitol Building at Washington D.C. (author)

Entering Washington, we are keen to see something of its iconic buildings and manage to spot the Capitol briefly before entering a long tunnel emerging in Union Station at around 09.30 hrs. We then pass through the heavily built-up areas of Maryland and Delaware, occasionally catching a glimpse of the sea before arriving in Philadelphia in Pennsylvania, arriving early. The train has to await a suitable 'path' on the track ahead and the conductor says we have about thirty minutes before departure, so we look at the impressive station building and concourse. I spot a new *Acela* train on test; due in service soon on *Metroliner* Washington-New York-Boston route at speeds up to 140 mph.

We leave Phildadelphia for the final ninety-mile journey to New York and pass through the heavily populated and industrialised New Jersey and, on the approach to Newark, get a brief sight of the New York skyline across the Hudson River before diving into a two mile long tunnel to emerge in Penn Station twenty minutes early. Given Amtrak's terrible timekeeping record, this is a 'red letter day' for them!

We thank our host and get a taxi to *Hotel Metro* on 35th Street, close to the centre of Manhattan. It has been booked for us by *Thomas Cook* and maintains the high standards we have come to expect. After settling in, I tell Josiane to get ready quickly as the light is fading but don't let on until we are outside the Empire State Building; en route we pass a *Day's Inn* and see our train host taking the sun outside the hotel. This is evidently her New York lodging and we don't know who is the most surprised! My reason for haste is so that we see the sun setting from the top of the Empire State though we have to queue for the lifts as there are so many people. When we reach the top, dusk is just falling and the sight is stunning; we see Manhattan lighting up and it's a rare kind of magic and a fitting end to a great train journey! We are to spend four days exploring this great city (Chap.15) before moving on to New England and eastern Canada.

     Big Easy   31 hours   Big Apple

Transcontinental trains grab the headlines and for good reason, after all they have a great pioneering history behind them and they're fun to travel on. With my travelling companions, I discover secondary routes which in many ways are more interesting, more intimate, often with older rolling stock and serving communities that depend on them as a lifeline. Alaska Railroad's *Aurora* includes stops where the train is 'flagged' by groups of hunters returning from a weekend in the wild.

The *Aurora* climbs steeply out of the valley near Nenana, Alaska (author)

So come on two journeys of exploration into the wild on trains of the Alaska Railroad and British Columbia Railway; and two more exotic itineraries in the Colorado Rockies and the Adirondack Mountains. The routes described are:

> The *Aurora*: Fairbanks to Anchorage, Alaska
>
> The *Caribou*: North Vancouver to Prince George, British Columbia
>
> The *Rio Grande Zephyr*: Salt Lake City, Utah to Denver, Colorado
>
> The *Adirondack*: New York to Montreal

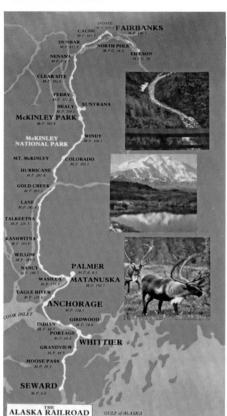

The lure of Alaska has been with Peter and me since our first visit to North America but remains in the 'too difficult' category until 1988 when we throw caution to the winds and decide on a sampler trip.

We share planning the itinerary. The flight to Anchorage and beyond is challenging; the air fares are high and flight options limited so we need to decide how long and settle on three days. The Alaska Railroad journey is a problem at this time of year with just one weekly train, out on Saturday and return on Sunday. I phone the railroad who are helpful, suggesting an air/rail package; it's surprisingly good value, flying out on Saturday evening, returning by train on Sunday. Our round trip starts with the flight to Fairbanks and on Sunday morning we join the *Aurora*, four coupled railcars, for the very scenic journey to Anchorage. The catering is simply a vending machine, so we stock up on sandwiches and beer. It leaves at 08.00 hrs for a 10½ hour schedule (it is to be 12 hours today); it is comfortable and warm, and the conductor offers coffee from his rear cabin for a donation of 50c per cup (being unofficial, he isn't allowed to charge). We aren't sure what to expect but the journey turns out to be one of the most amazing ever. Leaving semi-industrialised Fairbanks, we see little of modern civilisation for most of the day. After our stop at Nenana, I am invited into the front cab and learn just how different this railroad is; there are no fixed signals on the 350-mile route system!

The *Aurora*'s railcars are ready to leave Fairbanks on an epic 300 miles journey to Anchorage (author)

Priority is given to freight traffic which is a real lifeline for this vast and remote country and on arrival at refuge siding soon after Nenana, the train eases forward and reverses in to enable a freight train to pass on the same running line as we carry out the manoeuvre.

Left: a northbound freight train at Nenana passes our train after it has reversed into the loop (left, foreground). All contact is by radio and on sight. Note that there are no fixed trackside signals. As freight has priority, late running of passenger trains is endemic! (author)

The scenery is wild, beautiful and constantly changing through the river valley into the mountains at Healy where coal mining provides rail traffic for shipment through the port of Seward. On the way we spot the unique Dall Sheep native to this area. The train drops down to the high point of the trip, Denali Park whose station is gateway to the massive National Park (roughly the size of Wales). It's named after *Denali* the Inuit name for the highest peak in the USA (20,250 feet) formerly known as *Mount McKinley*. The train is on time and due to stop for 15 minutes so I get out for photos. After 5 minutes, the conductor signals departure and I scuttle back. Shortly after he comes up and in an uncompromising tone, says '*no matter the schedule, the train leaves when it's ready and if I hadn't seen you, it'd be a week to the next train, wouldn't that be just tough!*'

Mount Denali is somewhere in the clouds though we don't get to see its peak (author)

After leaving Denali Park station, we stop at stations interspersed with flag stops where intending passengers simply flag the train down from the lineside and we pick up at some of them; usually people go out on the Saturday train, hunt or whatever and return on Sunday, a unique service provided on this train. We are constantly on the lookout for *Mount Denali,* but high cloud persists in shrouding the summit (it has its own micro-climate) though we momentarily witness a lifting of the clouds. Talkeetna is a small town and base camp for climbers of the mountain, from where it's at least two day's march to the summit!

Right: weekend hunters who travel out on Saturday's train, return on Sunday at this 'flag stop'. Their 'luggage' consists of wild camping gear and boxes containing their 'catch' of local wild life (author)

Below: Hurricane Gulch, viewed from the train on the viaduct high above the frozen river (author)

Soon after, at Hurricane Gulch, it is standard practice for all trains to stop on its spindly viaduct for passengers to view the sort of scene that most people probably associate with the State: an icy and very cold landscape; it stays for several minutes to allow for photographs. The train steadily loses time as we head further south; freight trains given precedence at passing loops is standard practice and we hear that this train rarely does the journey in under 12 hours, today being no exception. Due to the late running, our next surprise is to see a 'switcher' locomotive has been called and comes from Anchorage to pilot the train for the rest of the journey. It moves towards us on the same track, stops, couples and proceeds, all under radio contact and sight. Our driver is relieved of duty as he must not exceed 12 hours driving under federal regulations. For an hour we are hauled by the switcher and arrive at Anchorage at around 20.00 hrs, after exactly twelve memorable hours on the train.

Right: journey's end; the *Aurora* arrives at Anchorage behind a relief locomotive. I am told that, due to precedence given to freight traffic, and the passenger train regularly late, so a switcher (shunting locomotive) is always on standby at Anchorage (author)

Left: the *Caribou* is one of my most amazing journeys: 465 miles and taking 13 hours from Vancouver through British Columbia's remote interior in a 1960's built rail diesel car. Here, the train is at the small town of Lillooet BC with another 300 miles to go to Prince George. It operates north of here just three times a week (author)

I am with Peter and pleasantly surprised to see the *Royal Hudson* excursion is still operating between North Vancouver and Squamish, ten years after my previous trip. I am invited to look over the footplate of the CN 6060 and amazed how high it is. We make the journey to Squamish and back in sunny weather, a pleasant contrast with 1978. We are up early next day for the 07.00 hrs *Caribou*, a through train on a 13-hour schedule to Prince George. Running Mondays to Saturdays, it does the whole trip three days a week, the other three to Lillooet. The train has four cars, two are to be dropped at Lillooet and return to Vancouver. It takes the same route to Squamish then into the mountains, passing through spectacular Checkaumus Canyon before arriving at the popular ski resort of Whistler. At Pemberton, one of our cars develops engine trouble, is detached and parked. From here the journey becomes very spectacular, hugging contours of the incredible Fraser River Canyon for miles. We arrive at Lillooet, the largest settlement, 165 miles from Vancouver and detach one car which will return to Vancouver that afternoon.

Left: the famous *Royal Hudson* steam excursion from North Vancouver to the small port of Squamish runs along the scenic Howe Sound on its 40 miles journey. Motive power is ex-Canadian National no. 6060, a powerful locomotive which once formerly headed transcontinental trains; it is assisted by a small freight locomotive (author)

It is not quite at the halfway point and from here on the scenery becomes heavily forested and I notice that most passing freight trains are loaded with packaged timber. There are three more mandatory stops in the next 300 miles and at each there is infrastructure for timber processing and loading.

Right: the spectacular Fraser River Canyon which is the highlight of this wonderful journey; the railroad track can be seen dropping down on the left and the gradient is quite steep. Weather conditions are not great this day (author)

At Williams Lake I spot a BC Rail locomotive still in original olive green whereas most now carry the new red, white and blue livery. Near Quesnel, the engineer alerts us to the presence of black bears at the lineside, and we are thrilled to see them scampering away from the train. We arrive in Prince George at 21.00 hrs after a long though not tedious journey and find a hotel near the station.

Left: the livery on BC Rail locomotives has recently changed to a cheerful red, white and blue. This train is conveying empty wagons for loading with packaged timber, mainstay of the state-owned British Columbia Railway. Its other staple traffic is coal from the inhospitable Tumbler Ridge field north of Prince George (author)

We rise to a fine day and an unremarkable town; the *Skeena* to Jasper leaves in the evening so we ask at the hotel what there is to do here, and the answer is *'not very much but even less today as it's a public holiday'*. We do some window shopping and then chance upon a garage renting a car for $1 just for this day plus 5 cents a mile, so we take it and explore the vast forest area north of here. In an interesting day out, we are hosted after lunch at a forest diner by its owner, Mrs Colquhoun, who hails from Sheffield. She takes us in her pick-up to look for bears; we don't see any, but I get a bonus when we visit her husband's logging haulage depot and start up (though don't drive!) a giant Kenworth truck (*right*).

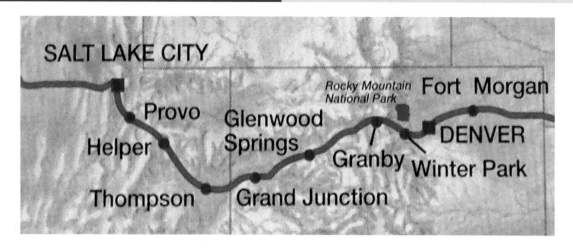

I travel this most iconic of routes three times, all in the same direction; in 1978 and 1980 on the *Rio Grande Zephyr* and in 1998 on the *California Zephyr* diverted from its Wyoming routing after the RGZ ceases operating. The journey description is of course the same.

The *Rio Grande Zephyr* at Granby, Colorado (author)

The *Zephyr* has fixed day and time schedules throughout its short existence. Never on Wednesday; east on Tuesday, Friday and Sunday; west on Monday, Thursday and Saturday; and always at 07.30 hrs for a 14-hour journey each way. Though a relatively short-distance train, it faithfully replicates the aura and facilities of the golden age of transcontinental travel.

My narrative relates to the 1978 trip. On boarding, we meet Douglas Ellison, Overseas Marketing Manager for British Rail, taking a couple of days out from his promotion of travel to the UK. He looks every inch an American, sporting a bright red shirt and check trousers; and travelling free around the States courtesy of Amtrak. It seems he has just paid full price for this train and is not best pleased when he learns that Paul and I have obtained the half-price concession available to visitors from outside the USA! The train's on-board facilities are superb, vista dome coaches, beaver tail rear observation car, a delightful dining car and attentive staff.

Left: the observation dome is one of the best features of the train and enables us to see both forward and side views of the dramatic landscape of the Colorado River Valley, Canyons and Mountains

Right: the dining car is well appointed with top notch service from a very professional team. There is an extensive menu with a wide range of meals, my favourite being the fresh Rocky Mountain Trout

Left: the rear facing bar lounge is excellent for relaxation and meeting other passengers. One is a young lady train buff who talks of her passion for model steam locomotives; it's a show stopper when she volunteers that her boyfriend has a *Big Boy*!

*The real *Big Boys* were a fleet of a 25 super-sized steam locomotives built in 1941 to haul massive freight trains over the mountainous route from Laramie, Wyoming to Ogden, Utah

(all photographs by the author)

Much of the journey is taken up with sightseeing; in a land of superlative train journeys, this has to be one of the best! The scenery is dramatic and varies from red cliffs and canyons in Utah, flat scrubland around Grand Junction and continual steep canyons between Glenwood Springs and Granby followed by a long climb to the famous Moffat Tunnel and steep winding descent on the Big Ten loop into Denver. We are amused by wacky junction names *Dotsero* (milepost 0) and *Orestod* at the other end of the new cut off. As is customary in the USA, we enjoy meeting many other passengers over lunch and in the bar. It is 21.30 hrs before the *Zephyr* arrives at Denver where we stay the night.

When Amtrak was created in 1971 from the dregs of a crumbling unprofitable passenger network, most train companies were only too glad to offload. Two companies, Southern Railway and Denver & Rio Grande Western opted to remain independent and maintain their reputation for good service. A third, Chicago, Rock Island & Pacific, a real no-hoper opted for independence and folded after a few years.

Above: the *Rio Grande Zephyr* near Bond, Colorado (author)

Below: the D&RGW is primarily a coal haulier: a very long coal train passes Hot Sulphur Springs, Colorado on a warm summer evening in 1978 (author)

The next time I travel this route is in 1998 by which time the independent *Zephyr* operation by the Denver & Rio Grande Western has long since been supplanted by Amtrak with its *California Zephyr*; a good train but lacking that unique quality touch! The Rio Grande is no more and the new owners, Union Pacific have diverted long-distance freight over their easier-graded Wyoming main line and freight service is reduced to relatively short-distance coal hauls.

Right upper: Grand Central Terminal, New York

Right middle: *The Adirondack* at Albany

Right lower: Montreal in the Fall

(upper and lower photos from shutterstock, centre photo by the author)

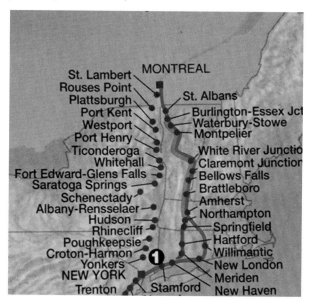

My very first train journey in the USA is made on the *Adirondack* as is my very last. In 1978, Paul and I travel from New York Grand Central Station and in 2000, Josiane and I travel from New York Penn Station. The route is the former *New York Central* to Albany and *Delaware and Hudson* north of there, thence *Canadian Pacific* to Montreal. It is 22 May that year and the timetable shows a train to Montreal leaving Grand Central at 12.30 hrs, so we take our bags to the station early to book our tickets. Had we not decided to do this, it could have been a disaster as Amtrak has recently retimed the train to 09.40 hrs and it's now 09.30. An altercation at the ticket office when we find out leads to us being advised to exchange our half price vouchers on the train.

The conductor can't do this and arranges enough time at Albany for me to go to the ticket office and I get the tickets after further words with a recalcitrant booking clerk. Despite not knowing where track 28 is in Grand Central, a station of two levels and 46 platforms, we find the said track and join the train, a 4-car Rohr Turbo with a minute to spare. Our first ever USA train journey is in a carriage with face-to-face seating, normal for us but quite unrepresentative of USA practice as we are to discover!

Catering is from an *Amcafé*, well stocked with food and drink in a confined area. The journey along the Hudson River valley to Albany is very attractive once out of the New York suburban area at Poughkeepsie and the train runs alongside the river with high cliffs either side of the valley; we pass the world-famous USA Military Academy at West Point before arrival at Albany. The trip along Lake Champlain is also very attractive and includes Fort Ticonderoga which I recall from my history books was an important place in the American War of Independence (maybe they beat the English at this point). All is well until a lengthy customs examination at the Canadian border causes an hour late on arrival at Montreal. We check into a hotel near Windsor station and the following day start our transcontinental journey to Vancouver.

It is September 2000 when Josiane and I set out from New York to Albany where we will rent a car and tour the New England states. Having come from New York on *Empire Service* to Albany a week before, we join

The journey by Lake Champlain is very attractive (shutterstock)

the *Adirondack* at 10.55 hrs for the journey to Montreal. On my first journey in 1978, I remember the long and tedious, border check at Rouses Point and have every reason for unease this year. When planning my holiday I discover that as my passport expires in November, the Canadian authorities might disallow entry unless I can prove I am going home before expiry. I have my air tickets but am still worried that some *jobsworth* at the border will turf us out; Rouses Point is in the middle of *nowhere*! Immigration officials come through and I spot backpackers being escorted off the train, not a comforting sight, but when they get to us, give the okay and carry on and I breathe a huge sigh of relief. One of the downsides of being on a train can arise when another passenger talks incessantly in a loud voice. We have one such, apparently, who is a student at university in New York and living in Montreal. We learn what he thinks about anything and everything; he doesn't like flying which is why he's on the train. He leaves at a suburb of Montreal to everyone's relief. Josiane describes him in French as a *je sais tout* (know-all). As we pull into Montreal's Central station, we spot the *Hotel Delta-Ville* where we are due to stay three nights. On arrival I find that our room overlooks the station; great! A few days later, we are on our final train of the holiday, the *Ocean* to Halifax, Nova Scotia.

18   Rio Grande Adventures

Silverton, Cumbres & Toltec and Galloping Geese!

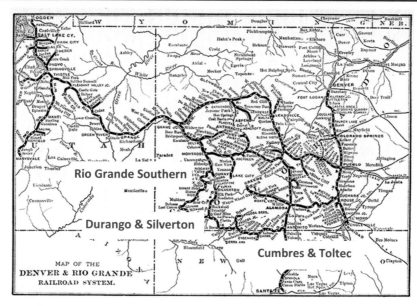

Map reproduced from Carstens Publications, inc.

Colorado memories of the narrow-gauge circle 1988

In the latter part of the 19th century, gold, silver and other precious metals were discovered in Colorado and spawned a system to transport them to market. It was to be a network of narrow-gauge railways, relatively cheap to build and operate; many companies were formed, the largest being the Denver and Rio Grande Western. As well as transporting metals, the railways became common carriers of all goods including livestock and later passengers. The doyen of passenger operation was the *San Juan Express* from Antonito to Durango which ran until 1951; It must have been a fascinating journey.

Two sections of the D&RGW are to be restored for leisure use, the Durango and Silverton in 1971 and the Cumbres & Toltec some years later.

Photographers' charter on the Silverton line (*Peter Duncan*)

Mikado 476 being prepared for the days' work at Durango depot (author)

In June 1980, we arrive in Durango for our ride on the famous Silverton line, the first of two sections of the Rio Grande narrow-gauge to make it into preservation. Our initial sight of the railway is two locomotives being prepared at Durango depot for the days' operations. The route is through the stunning Rockwood Canyon initially along the precipitous canyon wall high above a raging Animas River dropping down to the valley just feet above the river. We were to hear that later the following day, service had to be suspended due to flooding at this point.

High water on the Animas River; next day it bursts its banks and trains suspended (author)

Its name a giveaway, Silverton was of course a silver mining town and northern terminus of the original D&RGW network. Separated on the north and west by very high mountains, we hear about amazing Telluride just five miles to the west but separated by impenetrable mountains; we would like to go there but it has to wait for another time (Chap. 13).

On return to Durango, we pick up our car and travel north through Silverton (on a completely different route to that of the railway) then over the *'million dollar highway'* between Silverton and Ouray, so named because of the vast expense in building it to open up the silver mining towns to road transport (thus hastening the end of the D&GRW in the process!).

The train performs a 90 degree turn train above the precipitous Rockwood Canyon (author)

Eighteen years later, Josiane and I drop into Silverton on our journey south and later I find a vantage point on the hill above the town. There are four trains out on this day and I photograph one of them parked up awaiting the return.

Above: Two of the four trains this day waiting on the *wye* at Silverton before its return journey. What Americas call a *wye*, we call a *triangle*, where complete trains are turned; that is why American passenger cars have uni-directional seating (author)

I admit that I find the *Cumbres and Toltec* preferable to the *Durango and Silverton*, mainly because it looks and operates more authentically. It is 64 miles long, 19 more than the *Silverton* and trains are allowed nearly eight hours for the journey. The route is exciting with steep grades, wooden trestles, tunnels and the odd canyon.

We are in for a rare treat and are about to find this railway exceeds our high expectations. At breakfast, it is thrilling to hear the sound of a steam locomotive shunting the shed yard, its deep chime whistle blowing. Another locomotive is backing on to an 8-coach consist.

Mikado 497 shunts the coal stage at Chama (author)

The train is full of excited passengers including families; it is hauled by 488 and is soon off along the first few relatively flat miles before making the long and sinuous ascent of the 10,015 foot Cumbres Pass. Our journey is scheduled to almost 8 hours and the bus to get us back to Chama will take just over an hour.

Crossing the Lobito Trestle just outside Chama (author)

We are in no hurry and enjoy the sights and sounds of our steam locomotive working very hard. Once over the pass, the train drops down to the halfway point, Osier, which is in Colorado (in the 64 miles we cross the border between New Mexico and Colorado no fewer than eleven times).

Mikado 497 approaches the crossing point at Osier (author)

At Osier, we pass the westbound train from Antonito, hauled by another K36 *Mikado*. In an interesting manoeuvre, the locomotives continue, but the cars turn back and passengers are obliged to change trains. This takes an hour during which time, we go to a dining room and a meal of chilli con carne and rice is served (the meals are brought by van and reheated on the premises). After lunch, we are invited to look around the gift shop, where I purchase a fascinating book on the *Galloping Goose* story. The whole experience is clever marketing; we are captive with nowhere else to spend our money!

The famous Tanglefoot Curve, a double switchback (author)

Shortly after leaving Osier, we are in the dramatic Toltec Gorge, with several tunnels and high viaducts; from here, the line drops gently on to an Aspen covered plain and weaves in and out of adjacent states. In the warmth of the afternoon sun, it is a truly delightful experience to be riding in the rear open carriage; it is also less smoky as the locomotive drifts downgrade. We arrive at Antonito in late afternoon and notice that the connecting line to Alamosa and beyond is dual gauge; this is still in use for coal haulage and is part of the main D&RGW system. We pick up our bus connection and are back in Chama in a little over an hour.

The next day is warm and sunny and we have planned to chase and photograph the train from the lineside. Only the section up to the Cumbres Pass is accessible by road and it is also where the best photo opportunities are. We start at the famous Lobito Trestle, a wooden viaduct crossing Wolf Creek. The locomotive is making a lot of black smoke as the engineer opens her out for the climb ahead.

Keeping pace is relatively easy as, with the steep climb, the train isn't going very fast, so we are able to get quite a lot of photographs. Beyond the summit, where the line drops down towards Osier is the famous Tanglefoot Curve at Los Pinos CO; here the line does a double switchback making it possible to get multiple photographs standing on one spot and we take full advantage, photographing both eastbound and westbound trains in just over an hour.

Here, we say our farewell to the C&T line and head back to Chama, then south on the road to Sante Fe which we reach late afternoon.

The C & T train climbs out of Chama towards the Cumbres summit (author)

Although the *Denver & Rio Grande Western* was the dominant network in the Colorado Rockies, a number of smaller companies carved a niche for themselves in carrying the lucrative precious mineral ores. Prime among these was the *Rio Grande Southern*, operating between Ridgeway and Durango via Telluride and Dolores (connecting at both north and south ends with the D&RGW).

Nothing is left of this railway save for the track bed, remains of some stations, viaducts and tunnel, and the passenger depot at Telluride, restored as a craft beer brewery and restaurant. I am able to drive much of the way along its route which is in the most outstanding scenery imaginable, including the iconic *Lizard Head* mountain. This line was one of the most challenging and in the unforgiving territory in which it operated,

never made any serious money, closing in 1951 after a 60-year lifespan. In the early 1930's, RGS was in cost-cutting mode and looked at novel ways to convey passengers and mail more economically. Thus the *Galloping Goose*, a fleet of seven vehicles each with motor car chassis', cab and box container was introduced. The first hit the rails in 1931, and incredibly, six of these bizarre vehicles are in preservation. They operated for 18 years though in that

time, the mail contract was lost, and some *Geese* were converted for tourist travel. What a prospect for extreme tourism sitting in a cold, draughty box rolling and shaking over the sinuous route of the RGS! *It could be dangerous; in autumn 1935 a driveshaft snapped on one and severed the air line; without brakes,

it careers down the track, its passengers thrown out into a convenient snowdrift as the vehicle hits over 50 mph until stopped by trackmen laying chains across the line.

Top left: the spectacular *Lizard Head* with the former track bed visible in the foreground (author, all photographs)

Above: Goose number 2 restored, at rest in Telluride

Left: the sole remaining RGS depot, now a brewery and restaurant at Telluride, Colorado

(* *Tin Feathers & Gasoline Fumes* by Stanley Rhine, 1971)

Index and Appendices

Europe

Air France FR 22
Albi FR 19 35 37 38
Alcazar SP 58
Alhambra SP 61
Amiens FR 87
Andalucia SP 54 59
Ankarsrum SN 84
Antequera SP 59 60 61
Arctic Circle Express NO 86 91
Aubrac (L') FR 36
Auch FR 22
Aurillac FR 36 37
Auvergne FR 20 35
Avila SP 56 57
Bad Peterstahl GE 32
Bamberg GE 39
Barcelona SP 19 64 86 90
Bardot, Brigitte FR 30
Barr FR 33 34
Bavaria GE 39 40 42
Bergen NO 91 94
Berlevag NO 97
Berlin GE 52 79 80
Bernina Line SW 83
Black Forest GE 31 32 39 40 41
Bodo NO 91 94 95 98
Bologna IT 57 66 69 71 92
Bordeaux FR 23
Borscht 19
Bort les Orgues FR 37
Bratislava SL 51
British Airways Express 21
Brocken (the) GE 78 79 80
Brussels BE 15 32
Cadaques SP 54 64
Calais FR 7 8 20 87 88
Cannes FR 26 27 28
Cantal FR 22 37
Cardiff UK 21 22 101
Casa Montalbano IT 74
Castilla la Mancha SP 54, 55
Castilla y Leon SP 54 56
Catalan Talgo SP 86, 90
Catalonia SP 54 64
Catania IT 72
Cathars (the) FR 19 38
Causses Line FR 35 36
Cevennes Line FR 35
Channel Tunnel UK FR 15 88 166
Chemin de Fer de Provence FR 28
Chemin de Fer du Vivarais FR 76 77
Choucroute Garni 32
Chur SW 81
Cisalpin FR 86, 89
Ciudad Real SP 55
Ciudad Rodrigo SP 62
Clermont Ferrand FR 20 36

Colmar FR 31 32 33 34
Conquistadors SP 63
Cote d'Azur FR 9 24 87
Dali, Salvador SP 64
Dambach FR 34
Drei Annen Hoh GE 78 79
Dresden GE 14 80
Eiffel Tower Paris FR 43
Eisfelder Talmuhle GE 79
Erling Jarl (m.v.) NO 91 94 99
European Courts of Justice FR 31
EasyJet 14
Embraer Jet 21
Eurocity 89
Europabus 14
European Parliament FR 31
Eurostar 17 31 32 34 88
Extremadura SP 54 55 62 63
Fête des Citrons FR 26
Filisur SW 82
Flixbus 14
Fleche d'Or FR 86-8
Florence IT 66 68-71 86 92
Fragonard Parfumier FR 26
Franco dictatorship SP 54
Frankfurt Main GE 52
Frecciarossa IT 66 71 86 92
Frejus FR 24 28 29
Freudenstadt GE 32 40
Gernrode GE 79 80
Golden Arrow UK 86-8
Granada SP 59 60 61
Grand Canal IT 67
Grenoble FR 18 28 86 90
Grimaud FR 30
Guadalupe SP 62
Halberstadt GE 79 80
Hammerfest NO 97
Harald Jarl (m.v.) NO 96
Harwich UK 16
Harzquerbahn 78-80
Haut Koenigsburg FR 33
Havel, Vaclav CZ 53
Hell NO 8 91 99 143
Herald of Free Enterprise BE 17
Hof GE 39 40
Hofburg Palace AU 49
Honnigsvag NO 97
Hopkin, Mary UK 17
Hoogovens Steel NE 18
Horb GE 40, 41
Hotel Antica Badia, Ragusa IT 72
Hotel Formule 1, Caliais FR 20
Hotel l'Arena, Frejus FR 28
Hotel la Residencia Cadaques SP 64
Hotel Londra, Florence IT 69
Hotel Terminus Orleans, Paris FR 44
Hultsfred SW 85

Hurtigrute NO 93 94
Iberia Express 19
Iberico Ham SP 61
Inter-Rail 42
Irun SP 20
Italo IT 86 92
Jonjoping SW 84
Jetstream 41 UK 21
Kaiser Wilhelm FR/GE 33
Kinnock, Neil (Lord) UK 17
Kirkenes NO 94 97
Köln GE 13 78
Kong Olav (m.v.) NO 95, 99
Konstanz GE 41 42
Lago Bianco SW 83
Lake Vattern SN 84
Lamastre FR 76 77
La Tour de Carol FR 38 75
Lausanne SW 89
Le Cheylard FR 77
Le Mont-Dore FR 38
Le Puy-en-Velay FR 35
Le Treport FR 18
Ligne de Cerdagne FR 75
Lille FR 23 32 34
Lindau GE 42
Lofoten Islands NO 91 95 98
Loire Chateaux FR 16
London, UK 16-7 34 87-8 144
Lufthansa GE 52
Lutherstadt Eisleben GE 78
Luxembourg Gardens FR 45
Lynn, Dame Vera UK 95
Lyon FR 18 23 35 76 77
Madrid SP 54-56
Mafia IT 74
Manx Air UK 21
Marais, Paris FR 46
Marseille FR 15 16 28 36
Menton FR 7 16, 23-25 66
Merida SP 62 63
Midnight sun NO 96 97
Milan IT 15 40-1 66 71 86 92
Modica IT 74
Monaco FR 25
Montalbano (Insp fict) IT 72-74
Monte Carlo FR 24 25
Montmartre, Paris FR 46
Moors /Moorish SP 55 59 61
Narbonne FR 20
Narrow-gauge railways 75
Neath UK 7 16
Neuenmarkt-Wirsbg GE 39 40
Nice FR 23 25-28
Night Ferry UK/FR 16
Nord railway FR 87
Nordhausen GE 78 79
North Cape NO 97

Europe

Olympia GR	17
Orient Express	31
Oulu FI	17 19
Paella de Valencia SP	19
Parador SP	54 56 57 60 62
Paris FR	9 15-7 19-22 31 36 38 40 43
Pizarro, Francisco SP	63
Plaza Mayor SP	54 57
Polar bear NO	97
Polarlys (m.v.) NO	97
Ponte Vecchio IT	70
Porto PO	54 65
Prague CZ	43 44, 52-54 80
Prince Albert II FR	25
Prince Rainier III FR	25
Puertollano SP	55
Punta Secca IT	74
Putnik Travel Agency YU	21
Pyrenees FR/SP	75
Quedlinburg GE	80
Quixote (Monsignor fict)	56
Ragusa IT	8 72 73 74
Railjet AU	51
Reutte-in-Tirol AU	42
Rhaetian Railway SW	81-3 89
Riom-es-Montag FR	37
River Arno IT	69
River Danube AU	48, 83
River Douro PO	65
River Doux FR	76
River Inn SW	83
River Rhone FR/SW	76
River Vltava CZ	53
Rodez FR	21 35 37 38
Roissybus FR	22
Roman style SP	58 59 63
Rotary, Neath UK	8
Rottweil GE	40 41
Route des Vins FR	31-4
Sagrada Familia Barcelona SP	90
Salamanca SP	54 56 57 62
Salveson, Paul	84 85
Salzburg AU	51
Sami Lapland native SN	97
Schoenbrunn Palace AU	49
Scuols SW	14 82 83
Segovia SP	56 58
Seville SP	59 60
Sinagra, Balduccio (fict) IT	74
Siena IT	70
Smorgasbord NO	94-6
SNCF FR	10 36 76-7
Sound of Music (the)	51
Spanish Riding School AU	48
St Agreve FR	77
St Cirq Lapopie FR	35
St Etienne FR	35 77
St Marks Square IT	67
Ste Theresa of Avila SP	56
St Cirq Lapopie FR	35

St Etienne FR	35 77
St Marks Square IT	67
Ste Theresa of Avila SP	56
St Moritz SW	82 83
St Nectaire FR	22
St Pol s/Ternoise FR	17
St Raphael FR	28 30
St Stephens Cathedral AU	49
St Tropez FR	28 29 30
Ste Maxime FR	30
Stein, Rick	71
Stoomtren NE	18
Strasbourg FR	31-34
Stuttgart GE	40 41
Svolvaer NO	94 95 98
Swansea UK	23 34 101 164
Tarte Tropezienne FR	30
Thermal Express FR	38
Third Man (the) film	50
Three Musketeers (the)	22
Thusis SW	81
Tirano IT	82 83
Toledo SP	55 58
Torghatten NO	98 99
Tornio FI	17
Toulouse FR	19 20 35-8 64
Tour de France	20
Tournon FR	76-7
Tours FR	16
Train Ferry	17
Trabant car GE	78
Trams	10 27 45 49
Trans Europ Express	86 89
Trollfjord NO	96 98
Tromso NO	96 98
Trondheim NO	91 94 95 99
Trujillo SP	62-3
Uffizi Museum	69
Vastervik SW	83 84
Venice IT	10 43 66-7 71
Ventimiglia IT	24 66 87
Verona IT	66-7 71
Veynes FR	18
Viaduc de Garabit	36
Viaduc de Viaur	38
Vienna AU	20 43 48-51 80
Vigata (fictional)	72
Villefranche de Rouerge FR	36-7
Wernigerode GE	79 80
Westrail AU	51
Würzburg GE	39
Zeebrugge BE	17
Zernez SW	82

North America

Acadia Nat Pk ME	118
Adirondack (the)	198-9
Alamosa CO	203
Alaska Airlines AK	107-8 137
Alaska Marine Highway AK	93 137 183
Alaska Railroad AK	188-9

Albany NY	111 197-8
Albuquerque NM	122 159 175-6
Amtrak	100 104 106-8 119 127 133 155 162 171 174 181 184 195-6 198
Anasazi tribe NM	122
Anchorage AK	107-8 135-7 139 188-91
Animas River CO	200
Antonito CO	124-5 199 203
Arches Nat Park UT	120 123
Atlanta GA	185-6
Auke Bay AK	103
Aurora (the)	136 188-91
Bakersfield CA	130, 183,
Banff AB	163-4
Bar Harbour, ME	118
Bellingham, WA	100 137
British Columbia Railway BC	192-3
Big Bayou Canot AL	179
Black Canyon CO	125-6
Boston MA	105-6 109 111 115 148 153 168 187
Burlington Northern RR	155 171 173
Bridal Veil Falls CA	127
Broadway NY	151
Brooklyn Bridge NY	150
Broadway Limited	111 162 178 180-81
Buena Vista CO	121
Bush, George W	185
Cable Car CA	111 156-7
California Zephyr	123 126 162 171-3
Calgary AB	165
CalTrain CA	105 133
Cambridge MA	153
Canadian (the)	106 162-5
Canadian Pacific Railway	104 163
Canadian National Railway	104 165 192
Canadian Shield ON	164
Cantwell AK	139
Capone, Al	109 154
Captain Cook	136
Cardinal (the)	113 116
Caribou (the)	192
Carson City NV	116 128,
Chama NM	202
Charleston SC	108 148 160-1
Chattanooga TN	114
Chicago IL	105 109 111-3 123 148 154 162 169 171-2 174-6 178 180
Chicago Elevated Railway IL	154-5
Chicago, Rock Island & Pacific RR	196
Cimarron CO	125
Cincinnati OH	108 113 116
Coal Miners Daughter	114
Coast Starlight (the)	100 110-1 130 162 182-4
Coaster, San Diego CA	133
Colorado River CO	173 195
Columbia River OR	143 145 170
Concord NH	119
Conrail	111 181
Crescent (the)	162 185-7
Cumbres Pass CO	202-3
Cumbres & Toltec RR	123-4 179, 199, 202-4

North America

Cut Bank MT — 170
Daly City CA — 127 156
Dartmouth NS — 167 168 182
Death Valley NP CA — 127 129
Del Mar CA — 127
Denali Nat Park AK — 103 135 137
Denali Star — 139
Denver CO — 113 121 126 171-3 176 188 194
Denver & Rio Grande — 121-4 171 196 199 205
Desert Wind (the) — 112 113 127
Detroit MI — 106 109 113 154
Donner Pass CA — 128 172 173
Durango CO — 121-4 199-201 205
Durango & Silverton RR — 199-201
Eastwood, Clint — 125
Ellison, Douglas — 195
El Paso TX — 122 177-9
Empire State Building — 148, 150,
Empire Builder (the) — 112 141 162 168-9
Empire Service — 198
Fairbanks AK — 135 136 188-9
Fisherman's Wharf SF — 156-7
Flagstaff AZ — 120 175
Fort Sumter SC — 161
Fraser River CA — 128
Fraser River BC — 165 192-3
Fuzzy Bear — 140
Gershwin, George — 160
Georgetown CO — 121
Glendale CA — 116
Glenwood Springs CO — 121 122 195
Golden Gate Bridge CA — 157
Gore, Al — 110 185
Go Transit — 105
Granby CO — 194-5
Grand Canyon AZ — 120 175 177 183
Grand Junction CO — 120 123 126 172-3
Grand Teton Nat Park ID — 115 145
Green Mountains VT — 118 119
Greyhound — 11 100 108 119 141
Gunnison CO — 121 125
Gwenny's Kitchen AK — 136 137 140
Halifax NS — 112 166-8 198
Harlem NY — 150 153
Harrisburg PA — 181
Hill, James J — 169
Hoboken NJ — 105
Hoffman, Dustin — 108
Hot Sulphur Sprs CO — 196
Hudson River NY — 105 187 198
Hurricane Gulch AK — 191
Independence CA — 129
Indianapolis IN — 175
International Nickel Co. — 164
Jackson Hole WY — 115 145 147
Jasper AB — 165 193
Juneau, AK — 100-3 107-8 136-7
Kansas City MO — 112 175-6
Ketchikan AK — 101

Kindergarten Cop OR — 143
Klondyke Inn AK — 135 136
Keystone Service PA — 181
Lafayette IN — 113
Lake Champlain NY — 198
Lake Michigan IL — 154
Lake Shore Limited — 111
Lake Superior ON — 164
Lake Tahoe NV — 128
Lamar CO — 108 113 176
Las Cruces NM — 122
Las Vegas NV — 113 130 172
Lexington KY — 108 114
Lillooet BC — 192
Lizard Head CO — 205
Los Angeles CA — 109-13 147-8 174 177 182-3
MacLaine, Shirley — 12
Manhattan NY — 105 148-152 187
Mark Air — 108 135,
Matanuska (m.v.) — 100-1
Matapedia NB — 166
Medicine Hat SK — 165
Mendenhall Glacier AK — 137
Metra IL — 105
Mexican Hat UT — 123
Miami FL — 148 177-8
Mickey Mouse — 178
Midnight Cowboy — 108
Miller, Glenn — 113-4
Million Dollar Highway CO — 122 201
Milwaukee WI — 169 170
Minneapolis MN — 170
Mississippi River — 170 179 185-6
Mono Lake CA — 117 129
Monument Valley AZ — 120 122-3
Monroeville PA — 111 180-81
Montreal QC — 105 112 162-3 166 188 197-8
Mount Denali AK — 103 116 138-40 190
Mt Rainier Nat Park WA — 8 117 134 141-4
Mt St Helens WA — 8 111 170
Natchez Paddle steamer — 186
Nava-Hopi Tours AZ — 175
Nenana AK — 188-90
Nestucca Bay OR — 142
New Jersey Transit NJ — 105
New Orleans LA — 106 110 177-9 185-6
New York NY — 109-13 148-52 180 185-8 197-8
New York subway NY — 105 152
Northwest Airlines — 108 135 137
Oak Creek Canyon AZ — 120
Oakland CA — 113 130 133 156 171 172 182-4
Ocean (the) — 112 166-8 198
Oceanside OR — 142-3
Ogden UT — 145 147 172
Old Faithful WY — 145-6
Ontario Northland Rly — 164
Orlando FL — 177-8
Oroville CA — 128
Osier CO — 203
Ottawa ON — 106 164

Otter Crest OR — 142
Pacific Surfliner CA — 133
Palin, Sarah AK — 136
Paradise, WA — **8 117 134 141-4**
Peninsula Line — 105
Pennsylvania RR — 180
Philadelphia PA — 181 187
Phoenix AZ — 115 120 127 177-80
Pioneer (the) — 111 170 172
Pocatello ID — 112
Poncha Springs CO — 125
Portland OR — 141-2 169 170 183
Port of Tillamook Bay OR — 142
Prince George BC — 188 192-3
Porgy & Bess — 160
Puffin Inn — 136-7 140
Rail Runner NM — 159
Rand McNally Atlas — 181
Rio Grande Southern CO — 121 205
Rio Grande Zephyr — 122 194-6
Rockwood Canyon CO — 200-1
Rocky Mountains — 12 117 162-3 195 205
Rocky Mountain Nat Pk CO — 121
Rogers, Roy — 112
Rouses Point NY — 198
Royal Hudson — 192
Rutland VT — 119
Sacramento CA — 128-30 148 172 183
Sacramento Rail Fair — 127
St Louis MO — 113 154 176
Salida CO — 125
Salt Lake City UT — 111-2 172-3 194-5
San Antonio TX — 177 179
Santa Fe Southern RR — 159
Sea-Tac Airport WA — 135 137
San Diegan (the) CA — 127
San Diego CA — 115 131-2 184
San Francisco CA — 105 111 133 156-7 171 182-4
Sangre de Cristo Mtns CO — 124-5
San Joaquin CA — 130 133
San Jose CA — 105 130 182 184
San Juan Express CO — 199
San Luis Obispo CA — 182-5
San Ysidro CA — 131 132
Santa Barbara CA — 110 130 182-4
Santa Fe NM — 124 148 158-9 204
Sausalito CA — 157
Schwarzenegger, Arnold — 143
Seattle WA — 100 135 141 169 182-3
Sea Otters AK — 140
Sears Tower IL — 154
Seward AK — 136 140 190
Sierra Nevada CA — 116-7 127 129,
Silver Meteor (the) — 160 161
Silverton CO — 112 121 122 200-2
Sitka AK — 101 102
Southern Pacific RR — 127-8 130 182 184
Southern Railway — 185, 196
Southwest Chief (the) — 112-3 162 174-5
Space Needle, Seattle — 141

North America

Sparks NV	172-3
Spokane WA	170
Squamish BC	192
Stallone Sylvester	150
Staten Island Ferry	150
Statue of Liberty	150
Sting (the)	180
Stockton CA	116 130
Sudbury ON	164
Sunset Limited (the)	162 177-9
Swanzee NH	119
Talkeetna AK	116 138 190
Telluride CO	123-4 200 205
Texas Eagle (the)	177
Tijuana MX	132
Tillamook Bay OR	142
Times Square NY	109 151
Thunder Bay ON	164
Toronto ON	105 165
Trailways	108
Trivial Pursuit	111
Truth or Consequences NM	122
Turnagain Arm AK	135 136
Union Pacific RR	128 171 173 196
Vancouver BC	135 162-5 188 192
Via Rail Canada	104 106 163 165
Viewliner	186
Wardair	135
Washington DC	105-6 185-7
Western Pacific	171
Whitefield NH	119
Wild West outlaws	125
Williams, Tennessee	106
Winnipeg MB	164 165
Wolverine (the)	113
World Trade Centre NY	150
Wrangell AK	102
Yellowstone Nat Pk W	115 117 134 145-7
Yosemite Nat Park CA	117 133 157 184

North American States

AL	Alabama	185-6
AK	Alaska	100-3 134-40 188-91
AZ	Arizona	120-123 175 177-8
BC	British Columbia	188-192
CA	California	127-133 171-4 182-3
CO	Colorado	120-4 172-3 194-6 199-205
FL	Florida	177
GA	Georgia	185-6
ID	Idaho	145
IL	Illinois	154 155
KA	Kansas	176
ME	Maine	117-119
MD	Maryland	187
MA	Massachusetts	153
MS	Mississippi	179 186
MT	Montana	170
NV	Nevada	128 172
NH	New Hampshire	118-9
NJ	New Jersey	187
NM	New Mexico	120-4 159 178-9 203
NY	New York State	197-8
ND	North Dakota	170
ON	Ontario	164
OR	Oregon	141-3 169-70 183
PA	Pennsylvania	180-81
QC	Quebec	106
SK	Saskatchewan	165
SC	South Carolina	186
SD	South Dakota	8
TX	Texas	177-9
UT	Utah	120-2 173 195-6
VT	Vermont	118-9
VA	Virginia	185-6
WA	Washington	141-3
WY	Wyoming	145-7

European Countries

Austria	42 48 66
Czechoslovakia	51 52
East Germany	9 14 78
Finland	17 19
France	9 14 17-21 23 35 56 66 75 76 86-88
Germany	9 13 14 16 35 39-40 42 75 78
Greece	4 17 21 66
Hungary	9 21
Italy	9-10 14 23 57 66 71 83 86
Netherlands	9 16 18 66
Norway	16 86 91 93 94 98
Portugal	14 54 65
Russia	97 102
Slovakia	51
Spain	9-10 14 17 19-20 54 60 62 65
Sweden	75 84-85
Switzerland	9 14 31 42 75 81-83 89
UK	104 109 186 195
Wales	138 168 190
Yugoslavia	9 21 66

Transport Acronyms and Terminology

Amcafé	Amtrak buffet/dinette
Amfleet	Amtrak single-level car
AT&SF	'Sante Fe' railroad
Autorail	French diesel railcar
AVE	Spanish high-speed train
BART	San Francisco rapid transit
Big Boy	Union Pacific: World's largest steam locomotive
Cable Car	San Francisco rack tramway
CDG Paris	Charles de Gaulle airport
Corail	SNCF Confort-Rail
Daylight	Southern Pacific Trains
DDR	East German Democratic Republic
EMU	Self-propelled electric train
Galloping Goose	Rio Grande Southern rail-mounted station wagon
JFK	New York Kennedy Airport
LRC	VIA Rail Canada 'light rapid comfortable' train
Highball	Early USA signalling system
Mallet	Narrow-gauge articulated steam locomotive
Mikado	Steam locomotive of 2-8-2 wheel arrangement
Mountain	Steam locomotive of 4-8-2 wheel arrangement
Nohab	Classic Scandinavian diesel locomotive
Pacific	Steam locomotive of 4-6-2 wheel arrangement
Panoramique	SNCF tourist Autorail
PLM	Paris Lyon Mediterranee Railway
PO-Midi	Paris Orleans/Midi Railway
Rapide	SNCF express train
RATP	Paris Transport Authority
Roomette	USA luxury sleeper berth
RO/RO	Roll-on/Roll-off Car Ferry
Route 66	Iconic USA highway
Slumbercoach	USA budget sleeper berth
SNCF	French National Railways
Streetcar	American name for tram
Superliner	Amtrak double-deck inter-city passenger car
Talgo	Articulated tilting train with interchangeable axles
TEE	Trans Europe Express
TER	Regional express train (FR)
Thruway	Amtrak rail-link buses
TGV	Train a Grande Vitesse (FR)
UNESCO	United Nations Education, Scientific & Cultural Organisation
Vaporetto	Venetian Water Bus
Wagons-Lits	European Company for sleeping/dining cars

ACKNOWLEDGEMENTS

First and foremost is the debt I owe to my wife Josiane who inspired and encouraged me to write this book in the first place. Starting out as a series of annual travel logs, it soon became clear that it had the makings of a book and from that moment on, Josiane has been my constant supporter.

Second, I wish to acknowledge a number of close friends who accompanied me on my trips abroad between 1971 and 1993; since that date Josiane has been my companion to Europe and North America. I have permission to use their names (in the text as first names only) and they are:

Paul Collenette
Peter Duncan
Robert Thomas
Chris Taylor
Brian Thompson
Thank you all for being wonderful travel companions.

To Holly Hughes, Katie Jones (cover designer) and Michelle Smith of the Ouma Group in Swansea for marketing, publishing and design advice.

To Colin Speakman, long time friend and colleague, for putting together such a fine foreword and offering help and advice along the way.

To Nathalie Thomas for proof checking and lots of advice on layout and text.

To Isabelle Thomas for advice on marketing and promoting to the book trade.

To Stephen Miles for thorough and painstaking photo-shopping of sometimes badly degraded photographs

Photographs:
The majority of photographs are by the author
Those on pages 9 11 15 20 22 37 39 42 52 89 90 98 109 110 114 159 197 198 are from Shutterstock
Those on pages 107 182 184 are courtesy of Amtrak
That on page 199 is courtesy of Peter Duncan
That on page 16 is courtesy of Eastbank Model Railway Club
That on page 113 is courtesy of Jeremiah Cox
That on page 181 is courtesy of Conrail Historical Society
Unattributed photographs on pages 22 125

Printed by Gomer Press Ltd, Parc Menter, Llandysul, Ceredigion SA44 4JL

Cover: a montage of Hell Station, Norway and Mount Rainier National Park, Washington State USA
Frontispiece: Mount Rainier, WA (shutterstock)

Travel in North America

Through the Rockies on the Rio Grande Zephyr